# The Howling Man
By Lyn Murray

**Golden Panda Publishing**
USA

# The Howling Man

## Title Story
### A Collection of Strange and Terrifying Tales, Case Studies and More!

Adult Supervision Required

# Copyright

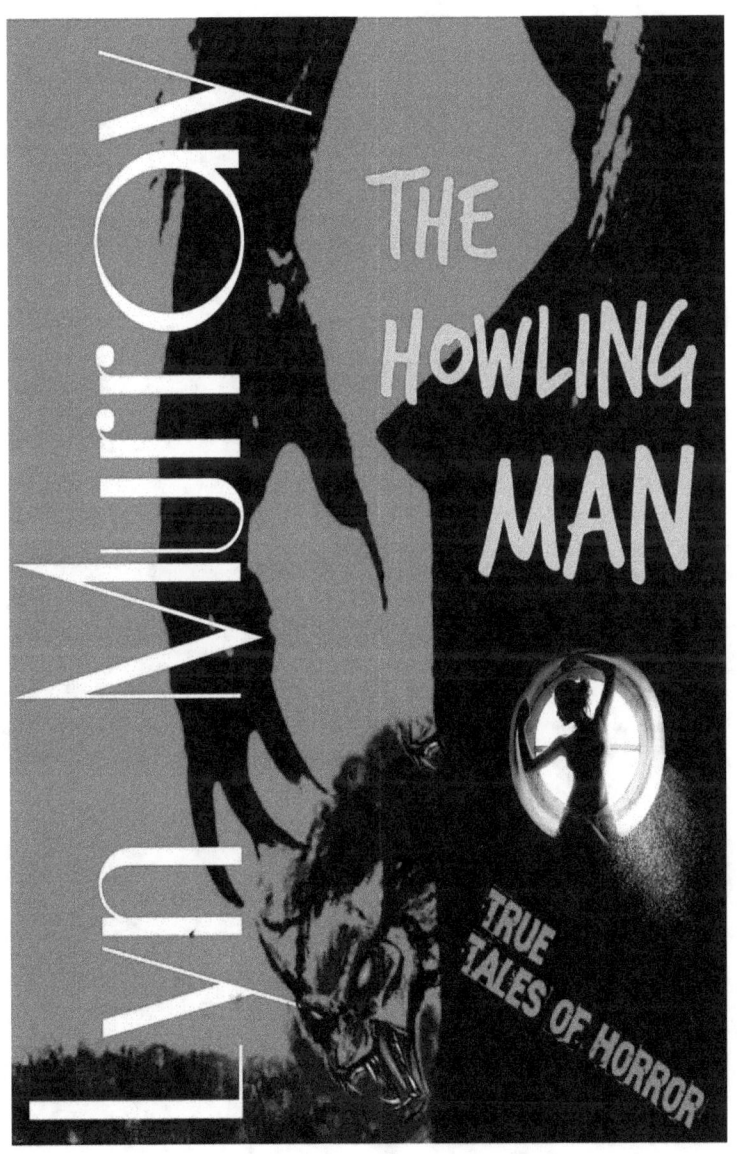

# The Howling Man

This is one great book for lovers of all things ***Werewolf!***

Lyn has compiled some of the greatest stories and information about werewolves ever told – including her own **The Howling Man**, which is based on actual events in Texas – that is sure to keep you up nights from here on out, with real case studies of "real" werewolves, historical legends, spine tingling classics that will have you on the edge of your seat – and a terrifying role playing game that you will never forget!

After teaching you, and scaring you to death – Lyn feeds you with some of her favorite recipes that are guaranteed to satisfy the Wolf inside. Lyn's delightful writing style is the literary equivalent of *"Dinner and a Movie"!*

So, settle back, and get ready for a *hairy* good time!

# Table of Contents

# 1

# Werewolves

# (Real Case Studies)

In this section, we will examine and discuss real case studies of real people who were considered Real Werewolves – and not all of them were men. That's right! Although not a popular subject – probably because of the supposed frailty of women, female werewolves are not talked about at any length. Or maybe it's just another male thing! Who knows? Anyway, we're going to talk about all kinds of werewolves here – and tell you some incredible REAL stories.

Dating back to Little Red Riding Hood (one of the best-loved children's fairy tales ever) the legend of werewolves has been with us. Did many take these tales seriously? Probably not; but I'm here to tell you, throughout history some cultures have taken them very seriously – to the point of hunting supposed offenders down, and killing them.

But it all began with Mythology!

## Classical antiquity

Zeus turning Lycaon into a wolf, engraving by Hendrik Goltzius.

A few references to men changing into wolves are found in Ancient Greek literature and mythology. Herodotus, in his *Histories*,[11] wrote that the Neuri, a tribe he places to the north-east of Scythia, were all transformed into wolves once every year for several days, and then changed back to their human shape. In the second century BC, the Greek geographer Pausanias relates the story of Lycaon, who was transformed into a wolf because he had ritually murdered a child. In accounts by the *Bibliotheca* and Ovid (*Metamorphoses* , Lycaon serves human flesh to Zeus, wanting to know if he is really a god. Lycaon's transformation, therefore, is punishment for a crime, considered variously as murder, cannibalism, and impiety. Ovid also relates stories of men who roamed the woods of Arcadia in the form of wolves.

In addition to Ovid, other Roman writers also mentioned lycanthropy. Virgil wrote of human beings transforming into wolves. Pliny the Elder relates two tales of lycanthropy. Quoting Euanthes, he mentions a man who hung his clothes on an ash tree and swam across an Arcadian lake, transforming him into a wolf. On the condition that he attack no human being for nine years, he would be free to swim back across the lake to resume human form. Pliny also quotes Agriopas regarding a tale of a man who was turned into a wolf after tasting the entrails of a human child, but was restored to human form 10 years later.

In the Latin work of prose, the *Satyricon*, written about 60 C.E. by Gaius Petronius Arbiter, one of the characters, Niceros, tells a story at a banquet about a friend who turned into a wolf. He describes the incident as follows, "When I look for my buddy I see he'd stripped and piled his clothes by the roadside... He pees in a circle round his clothes and then, just like that, turns into a wolf!... after he turned into a wolf he started howling and then ran off into the woods."

So, yes, Lycanthropes has been and is likely to

be with us – forever!

Before we begin our very own personal werewolf story, we're going to examine ten or so very famous cases (most of which happened a long time ago) with one exception - The Martin Case, that's sure to stop your heart a time or two. But, first, the old ones.

**Now, let's examine the case of** Gilles Gamier –

Back in the sixteenth century, in the town of Dole, townsfolk decreed by proclamation that anyone with the wherewithal could (and was invited to) hunt down and kill a werewolf that had been terrorizing the village.

As the story goes, one day while walking in the forest, a group heard a small child screaming for its life and naturally, they rushed toward the screams to render aid. When they arrived, to their horror, they saw a wounded child fighting off a monstrous creature – which they later identified as one Gilles Gramier. Later on, when a young lad of 10 disappeared in the vicinity of Granier's home, he was arrested, and did confess to being a werewolf!

The sentencing and judgment was swift: he was burned at the stake – probably on the town square.

## The Greifswald Werewolves:

According to the oldest of records, c. 1640, the German city of Greifswald was overrun with werewolves. Reports say the situation was so dire, that townsfolk were afraid to venture out after dark. Many brave souls that did – were never seen again.

Local students (being young and foolish) decided to take it upon themselves to rid their community of the blight and gathered up anything that was silver, which they melted down and rendered to bullets.

Records indicate a killing spree ensued – which supposedly rid the town of the pesky werewolves. Only a few students were lost!

## The Werewolf of Ansbach:

Supposedly, a dead mayor returns as a werewolf. (No wonder he wasn't reelected – he ate the voters!)

Those who know say that in 1685, in the Bavarian town of Ansbach was being set upon by a large, vicious wolf. Townsfolk claim it was their dead mayor. One can't help but wonder why?

Anyway, they tracked the wolf down, killed it and hanged it – but not before dressing the beast in clothes to resemble the Mayor. Talk about 'truth being stranger than fiction'!

When they were tired of looking at the rotting corpse, they transferred the monstrosity to a museum.

### The Klein-Krams Werewolf:

This tale borders on the supernatural. Rumor has it that the woods around Klein-Krams, near Ludwigslust, Germany, was teaming with all kinds of desirable game, and hunters near and far would gather there, and have 'a killing good time'.

However, there were reports that all sportsmen (at one time or other) reported seeing a huge wolf – that escaped all bullets. The beast was said even to taunt the hunters by coming close enough to steal their game, before running off into the woods.

One day, during one of these famous hunts, a

young Calvary officer was traveling through town, when a group of people came running and screaming out of a nearby house. When he failed to see anything chasing them, he stopped one of them and asked what the problem was. The child proceeded to tell him that the young Feeg son (who'd been left alone in the house they were visiting) had transformed himself into a werewolf and tried to attack them.

Of course, the officer didn't believe him (would you?) but while he was laughing he caught glimpse of a wolf running through the Feeg's house. When it stopped in front of a large window and promptly turned into a boy – he stopped laughing!

**Werewolf of Pavia:**

This one is a good lesson in 'knowing when and when not to stir things up – and knowing when to keep your mouth shut!

Back in 1541, Pavia, Italy, a farmer (as a wolf) fell upon many folks in the country and tore them to pieces. After causing townsfolk untold trouble, he was caught. When confronted about his maniacal carnivorous ravings (after being told he didn't look like a wolf) the farmer exclaimed, "The only difference between me and a wild wolf, is that I'm hairy on the inside."

You can guess the outcome – to prove the farmer right, the townsfolk proceeded to dismember, and disembowel him in search of his hairy insides. Of course – he didn't live to tell the tale.

**The Werewolf of Chalons:**

One of the worst ever werewolf stories comes out of Chalons, Paris on December 14, 1598, about a crazy tailor who lured children into his shop, where he killed them, powdered and dressed then, and displayed them as butcher's cuts of meat, and cut up their flesh into the shape of wolves. Society was so appalled by his behavior that even his real name is lost to history.

Late at night, he was said to roam the town, jumping out at passersby and ripping their throats out.

Upon his death, barrels of bleached bones were found in the cellars of at his shop. They say he was unrepentant and blaspheming to his very last breath!

**Claudia Gaillard, Werewolf of Burgundy:**

This took place during the Witch Trials – so who knows if any of it is true; but rumor has it that Claudia was seen turning into a werewolf (without a tail) and was taken into custody and withstood the horrors of questioning. It is said that Henry Boguet (witch hunter extraordinaire) couldn't break her – no matter what torture he exacted against her. After undergoing untold torture, she was burned to death at the stake.

**Michel Verdun, Werewolf of Poligny:**

In 1512, Jean Boin, Inquisitor of Besancon, tried Montot, Pierre Bourgot, and Michael Verdun for having made a pact with the devil – and for lycanthropy. These three men became known as – the werewolves of Poligny.

The three men came under suspicion, when a wolf attacked a passing traveler. While he was defending himself, he wounded the animal, which caused it to retreat.

After the attack, the traveler tried to find help, and came upon a hut, where he found a woman tending a wound in her husband's side. Believing this poor man was the human form of the wolf that attacked him, he notified authorities – and the rest is history. Of course, they tortured him – and he confessed to being a shape-shifter, and promptly named two friends as accomplices. (They probably owed him money. So much for friendship.)

**Benandanti Werewolves:**

This is an example of 'quick thinking' that probably saved this man from being burned at the stake.

This case was actually tried in Jurgenburg, Livonia, situated in the area east of the Baltic Sea, when an 80-year-old man named Theiss was tried for being a werewolf.

Theiss confessed to being a werewolf, and told the court that he and his friends were 'Hounds of Heaven', fighting the evil of witches from putting blight on their crops. He said that he and his brother hounds went underground (to hell) to fight the witches, to keep them from surfacing and killing the crops.

How can you burn a guy at the stake for helping God, right?! Right! Theiss was sentenced to several lashes and set free!

Like I said, fast thinker. Theiss can bat for my team any day!

**The Case of Jean Grenier:**

During the early spring of 1603, a reign of terror spread through the St. Sever districts of Gascony, in the extreme south-west of France (department of Landes).

Babes were snatched from their cradles, no one was safe inside or out, people's throats were torn out, and townsfolk were missing. One young girl escaped certain death and fled to local authorities.

Werewolf was on everyone's mind and tongue.

When a young boy of 13 was found boasting of his wolfish kills, and tales of the young girl fighting him off with a stick – well, it isn't known what happened to him, but it's a safe bet he didn't fare well!

**And now – the Martin Case, Palmyra, Maine:** (22nd Century – that is to say . . . today, 2013!)

This one is guaranteed to keep you up nights. After reading it, if you have any backbone left – The Howling Man (our title story) will render it to mush!

The Martin's new country home sat at the edge of a dense forest. One night – while sitting on their front porch, their dogs became excited and fearful, cowering at the slightest sound.

Getting up to see what troubled them, the husband and wife noticed strange stirrings in the nearby woods, and found 5 (yes five) sets of glowing eyes peering at them from the forest's edge. The exact same direction the dogs were looking to, and shrinking from.

Startled yes, but it wasn't until the creatures stood up and started walking toward them on two legs (like a human) that they really became afraid. Scared, they decided to go in and take the dogs with them. The minute the dogs were in the house, they took shelter and disappeared.

The Martins began locking up the house, when Mr. Martin decided it might be safer to get his family out of there – so he grabbed the truck keys and headed out the door to bring the truck closer to the front.

When he reached the truck, he dropped the keys, so he bent over to pick them up. When he stood back up to unlock the door, reflected in the truck's driver's side window was a towering werewolf standing right behind him.

If the security lights hadn't come on and scared the beast away – he would not have survived to tell the tale.

Driving the truck to the front of the house, he jumped out and ran back inside to get his family – but it was too late, the werewolves were upon them. The Martin's called local police for help, but they didn't believe them, and just told them to lock up and stay inside for the night. Which is what they did.

The morning couldn't come fast enough, and when it did, the Martin's fears were realized, as they slowly ventured outside to find the damage done by their unwanted guests, rendered by claw marks no human could have made!

It's reported that they moved back into the city. *I don't blame them!*

### The Martin House
## Palmyra, Main

12) The Beast of Brey Road –

The **Beast of Bray Road** (or the **Bray Road Beast**) is a cryptid, or crypto zoological, creature first reported in 1936 on a rural road outside of Elkhorn, Wisconsin. The same label has been applied well beyond the initial location, to any unknown creature from southern Wisconsin or northern Illinois and all the way to Vancouver Island, Canada, that is described as having similar characteristics to those reported in the initial set of sightings.

Bray Road itself is a quiet country road near the community of Elkhorn. The rash of claimed sightings in the late 1980s and early 1990s prompted a local newspaper, the *Walworth County Week*, to assign reporter Linda Godfrey to cover the story. Godfrey initially was skeptical, but later became convinced of the sincerity of the witnesses. Her series of articles later became a book titled *The Beast of Bray Road: Trailing Wisconsin's Werewolf.*

The Beast of Bray Road is described by purported witnesses in several ways: as a bear-like creature, as a hairy biped resembling Bigfoot, and as an unusually large (2–4 feet tall on all fours, 7 feet tall standing up) intelligent wolf-like creature apt to walk on its hind legs and weighing 400-700 pounds. It also said that its fur is a brown gray color resembling a dog or bear.

Although the Beast of Bray Road has not been seen to transform from a human into a wolf in any of the sightings, it has been labeled a werewolf in newspaper articles.

◇◇◇

And now ... if you're ready ...

# 2

## The Howling Man

## Introduction

*The story you are about to read is taken from true and mysterious events that remain unexplained to this very day. As per their request, we have changed the names of the family involved to protect their privacy; and we thank them for graciously allowing us to share it with you.*

*This horrifying story is relayed to us by Jim – the oldest lad, now grown and remembering.*

*On a day – not unlike today, a family sets out to visit relatives who live in the country, something they've done dozens of times; but today will prove to be like none other, when they are unexpectedly thrust into the heart of terror by something they cannot see. An encounter that not only changes their perspective of reality but their lives – forever!*

*Now I give you –The Howling Man.*

# The Howling Man
by Lyn Murray

## *(A True Story)*

## Chapter 1

We were spending the night at our grandparents' house. Mom and Dad, and we three kids, me, my brother Josh, and sister Cindy. It's not something that we often did, but still managed on a fairly regular basis, about every six months or so. Usually on a long weekend, we'd load up the car and drive three-hundred miles to Grandma and Grandpa's house in the country where we'd spend the night and rest up before heading home. Because we lived so far away it was nice to rest up, and staying the night gave us time to see all the relatives that lived nearby, and catch up on gossip.

Grandpa fancied himself a chef and loved to cook out, and he always fixed a spread fit for kings. And all the neighbors were invited, all the ones that lived nearby. About four families.

Grandpa's spread was pretty typical, he'd barbeque chicken, slabs of ribs, pork, and beef, and use his "secret sauce" (which was anything *but* typical) on everything but the roasted ears of corn – which he'd of smeared down too, if Grandma hadn't stopped him.

While barbeque wasn't Grandma's forte, her mustard potato salad was worth fighting for – so that was always her contribution by popular demand. Various neighbors, aunts, and uncles would bring their favorite dishes too – so there was plenty to eat! I'm telling ya, by the time the table was loaded up with food – it was a feast to behold!

I remember that Grandpa had a sixteen-person picnic table in the backyard that he made himself, but it was big enough for twenty, at least. Still, and just in case there were more people than seats, the neighbors always brought extra folding tables and chairs with them.

It was the best time whenever we visited, and we always hated to leave. *But that was about to change.* This night would change *a lot of things*, especially the way we all felt about country living (which we had loved because getting away from the city was so relaxing); but after the event that were about to unfold – we decided that farm country was just too isolated from civilization.

## Chapter 2

I usually stayed outside with Grandpa while he fired up the cooker and got the meat started. I'd fetch him wood, and whatever else he needed. We always enjoyed this time; it was *Our time*. Time to talk about whatever we wanted. *Private talk*. Grandpa always had something to confess – a secret he'd been hiding from Grandma. Usually, I had a secret or two myself that I was dying to share with someone whom I knew wouldn't tell. *You know, guy stuff – and Grandpa was my man!*

Along about 6 P.M., all the invited ones started showing up, and all the women gathered in the backyard to set up the picnic table with plates and food. Along about this time, Grandpa would usually go inside, but I always stayed behind to sneak a bite before supper. *And I always got caught!* When I'd go inside complaining to Grandpa, he'd laugh and tell me I should know better by now. Nodding yes, I'd go wash up for supper, and then rejoin Grandpa in the living room, where I'd always find him watching the news on the TV.

Around 6:30 P.M., everyone started venturing outside and gathering 'round the picnic table. By 7:30 P.M. we were all so stuffed we could hardly move; but there was clean up to do, and nobody got to go inside until the picnic table was cleared, the garbage was collected, and the leftovers were stored in the refrigerator.

By 8:00 we were all inside, except for a few stragglers who stayed behind to scarf down any remaining tidbits on their plates. Of course, we kids would gather around the TV making sure we controlled the channels so some adult wouldn't come in and tune it to something boring, while most of the grownups chose up sides and gathered around card tables for stiff domino competition. By 10:30 P.M., everyone was getting pretty tired; and one by one, the invited ones began to leave.

While Grandma fixed sleeping pallets for us kids on the living room floor, we dressed for bed. By 11:30 or so, even the grownups were fast asleep.

That night we couldn't have been asleep long when we were startled awake by a blood-curdling howl coming from outside. Even though it sounded far away, it was still loud enough to wake the house and give everyone a start. All us kids jumped up just in time to see the grown-ups rushing into the living room to check on us. Once they were assured we were okay, they began to question each other about – *that howl.*

*And there it was again. Louder this time. And piercing!*

Grandpa briefly looked out the front window (pulling together the heavy drapes), while Dad headed to the kitchen to make sure the back door was locked. When he rejoined us in the living room, he found us huddled together on the couch, away from the living room's big picture window; even now, even after all this time, I remember wishing that window was smaller. Funny how you remember little details like that.

*And there it was again!*

*Even louder.*

*And closer!*

How close was hard to determine. In the country, it's hard to tell distance because of the openness, but it definitely – *was* – closer.

It was then that Dad and Grandpa decided to walk the house to make sure all the windows were locked. I followed and lagged behind and stood in the archway that separated the living room and dining room. Dad and Grandpa didn't even know I was there, and when I overheard Dad whisper to Grandpa that whatever that thing was . . . *it was huge,* and it sounded either wounded or crazy and if it decided to break in the house – they're be no way to stop it – *I wished I hadn't been.*

And after hearing what I was never meant to, I somberly rejoined my family in the living room (hoping the fear in my heart wasn't noticeable on my face because they'd ask what was wrong, and I didn't want to scare them any more than they already were) and quietly huddled with them on Grandma's soft, leather couch. And although I wanted to scream – *let's get out of here*, I never said a word and waited for my dad and Grandpa to return to us.

When they returned, Dad grabbed a couple of chairs from around the dining room table for him and Grandpa and sat them in front of the couch. It was the strangest reunion because none of us spoke a word and just sat there looking at each other, *as if waiting helplessly for whatever came next – knowing something would!*

When Grandpa wondered if we should call the neighbors and tried to dial out – he got a funny kind of busy signal. Knowing we'd be afraid, he looked around at us comfortingly (attempting to instill confidence and assure us that everything was going to be OK), saying, "It happens. We're on a party line and sometimes you just can't get a clear line out. Not to worry," he said, "I'll try again a little later."

And just when I had begun to believe everything would be OK and relax a little – *there it was again! Even closer still!*

"Dad?" Near panic, I grabbed the sleeve of Dad's robe. "Dad – what is that?"

"I don't know son, but we'll be okay as long as

we stay here."

The look on my face must have conveyed the dread of another scenario because he repeated himself, this time more firmly, "We'll be fine son. Just remain quiet."

With that, Cindy began to cry, so Mom pulled her closer. Josh didn't cry, but he snuggled closer to Grandma. I was too big to snuggle. At eight you don't snuggle, *but I sure felt like hiding under the covers and would have but I was too afraid to move.*

And then the house shook, I mean really shook – as if someone grabbed it and ripped it off its foundation and shook it as hard as they could.

"Dad!" *I stood up!* "Dad!," I said, turning around, looking to the kitchen, my eyes locked in place, locked on that dark space, looking past the darkness into the darkness of my mind while imagining the horror outside. Unable to move, somehow able to speak, I whispered, *"It's in the backyard."*

"It's okay son; it's just the wind," Dad said, as reassuringly as he knew how.

With my eyes still locked in place, I

44

whispered, *"Are you sure?"*

Dad took my arm, and gently squeezing it, said, "Yes son, I'm sure. It's just the wind."

*Funny, I thought to myself, I didn't hear any wind a moment ago; but I was so scared and wanting this to be over that I would have believe Dad if he'd said it was a tooth fairy with really big wings!*

And there it was again! And it *was* – in the back yard.

**"Dad!"** This time I grabbed his arm with both hands and seeing the panic in my eyes, Dad reached out and firmly grabbed both of my arms and told me to stay put, "Jim – stay here. Stay with your Mom."

And pushing me into my mother's waiting arms, He and Grandpa hurried to the kitchen and disappeared into the unsure darkness they found there.

It was dark where we were too, except for the flickering light coming from the fireplace. I remember how their shadows cast unearthly figures on the wall as they rushed past it, conjuring up all kinds of images I didn't want to think about, much less see.

And they no sooner had disappeared into the dark kitchen when a howl – *more like a growl* – ripped through the house as if whatever made it was standing right in front of us.

*I can't relay the fear I felt, it was as if lightning struck my heart, and I'm sitting there thinking, was it – in the house?*

## Chapter 3

I called after Dad with a small *under-the-breath* sort of voice, *"Dad!"*

With a forced whisper emanating from the dark kitchen, Dad unwaveringly instructed me to stay there, "Jimmy, don't leave your mother."

Unable to contain my fear, nor heed mother's strong urging to remain calm, I replied, *"Dad! It's in the house."*

He quickly countered, I think hoping to belay my fears, "No son, it's not in the house. *It's in the backyard!* The chickens are going crazy."

Unsteadily I asked, ". . . You see it?"

"No son — just where it's been."

*I wouldn't understand what that meant 'till dawn, until I saw for myself, where it – had been.*

***"Where – it's – been?"***

However, before the words had barely left my mouth, another blood-curdling howl coursed through the house! Then there was a loud bang, and the house shook again. *Something had been thrown against it. But what?*

Fairly panicked now, I shouted, "Dad! Dad!"

Pulling away from my mother and statically charged – I ran into the bleak kitchen to find Dad and Grandpa peeking around the curtain that was covering the window on the back door.

When I shrieked, *"What is that?"*

*Grandpa reached out, grabbed me, and held me tight, while hissing,* **"Shhh.** Don't make a sound. It might hear us."

*I don't know why, but I glanced at the kitchen clock on the wall beside the pantry. It was a little after midnight. I don't know what difference knowing that made, except for making me wish that it was already morning.*

When a brief moment of silence followed, the three of us stood there by the back door (frozen in our tracks) afraid to move, afraid to speak all the while fearing the next moment to come.

And come it did with a BANG!

Again and again, the howling man screamed, banged and hit the house. *Again and again!* It went on for hours and hours, finally stopping around four in the morning.

We were so anxious to see the outside, to see what damage had been done, but we weren't about to go out 'till dawn. Not until it was good and daylight. And waiting for daybreak, so tired and scared and afraid to be far away from each other, we spread out the pallets Grandma had made into bigger pallets – so everyone could lay together on the floor beside the fireplace.

The remainder of the night Grandpa and Dad stayed awake, kept watch, and kept the fire stoked. I couldn't sleep either, and kept silent vigil – with one eye on the front door, and the other on the dark kitchen that this night had transformed into an unrecognizable, otherworldly black hole of despair, forever tainting me from seeing it as a place to have warm cozy breakfasts with my family.

And there, transformed by fear and silently locked within our thoughts – we waited for sunrise!

At first light, Grandpa and Dad began preparing to venture outside. I wanted to go, but they wouldn't let me until they knew it was safe. I guess they finally ended up going out back around six. Living in the country, Grandpa always kept his shotgun handy for coyotes – they loved raiding the hen house. Still, he rarely ever took it out of the gun cabinet; *but this morning, he would not be leaving the house without it.*

*The chickens.* Suddenly I wondered if the chickens were okay? I guessed we'd soon know. Funny, that's the first time I'd really thought about the chickens since last night.

I locked up the back kitchen door after Dad and Grandpa went outside. We all watched them through the kitchen window as they searched for clues about our late night visitor. It was scary watching them search the yard. Even though things had been quiet enough for several hours, the thought of them going outside was still chilling. We had the house to protect us. *They were out in the open with nothing to protect them.*

When Grandpa signaled all clear (at least from the house to the barn) we were relieved. While we hated to see them go in there – we knew they had to. As we watched them, we held hands so tight that our fingers went numb. Our hearts sank to the floor when Grandpa suddenly came running from the barn waving his arms in the air like a madman. We just knew something horrible was wrong. But running toward the house he waved us outside, shouting, "It's okay, come on, Y'all have to see this."

I don't know who turned it first, but we all reached for the doorknob at the same time, and the next thing I remember we were out the door and onto the porch and into the yard – *headed for Grandpa.*

Surprisingly, there wasn't as much damage as expected. A few planks of wood were scattered about, Grandma's Peach Tree had taken a hit, and the picnic table was turned upside down, but nothing else to speak of.

*Nothing we immediately recognized – anyway.*

But when Grandpa took Grandma's hand to lead us into the barn we knew we were in for an astounding discovery because he began to prepare her for what was inside.

"Now, mother, I don't want you to get too upset," he said, "some of our chickens have been killed, but as bad as that is, what I'm about to show you is worse."

*I remember wondering how anything could be worse than dead chickens. I was a blink away from finding out.*

When Dad came through the chicken house door and back into the barn, his eyes were wild. Shaking his head in disbelief, he said, "It's messy in there, but if you think you can stand it – *you need to see this.* . . . Everyone okay with it?"

Mama thought it best that she and Cindy stay where they were. *Not me!* I had to see. So grabbing Josh by the hand we followed Dad, Grandma and Grandpa into the chicken house.

There were feathers and chicken bodies everywhere! *You couldn't step without stepping on one. Whatever this was, it was no coyote – I thought to myself.* Then dad pointed to the back wall of the chicken house. *It was gone! I mean completely gone.*

And then he led us to the back of the chicken house – through the hole where the wall had been, and to the back of the barn. We found splinters of wood and chicken feathers scattered in a hundred places behind the barn; but what we couldn't take our eyes off, what we would never be able to explain, *OR forget*, were the huge claw marks just below the roof of the barn that trailed the wall from roof to ground.

Whatever made those marks had to be fifteen feet tall. *Or taller!* Whatever made those marks was bigger than any coyote I ever saw, and no coyote I ever heard . . . *howled like a man.* **No!** Neither the largest wolf nor Puma could do this.

*After hearing what we heard . . .*

*After seeing what we'd seen . . . there was only one conclusion.*

We all looked at each other. The unspoken truth was written across our faces with undisputed clarity. At that moment, whatever we thought we knew – *went flying out the window with our sanity.*

While we would never know exactly what had visited us, we knew three things for sure . . .

*One – Whoever . . . Whatever our visitor had been – it was big!*

*Two – it was no animal we knew of.*

*And three – and perhaps the most terrifying realization of all (and there wasn't a doubter among us) whatever our visitor was, it most definitely was not – human!*

∞

*Whatever anyone else might think, I know it wasn't human – because I still have the one and only clue found the next morning locked tight inside my toolbox. A clue that I never shared with my family – didn't want to scare them. But I still have it, and sometimes I unlock the box and take it out, and remember how lucky we are to be alive, how lucky that I only found it stuck in the wood of the old chicken house (and not in my throat) – that eight inch gnarly claw still stained with blood that changed my life – forever!*

*I still have it!*

*Would you like to see it?*

◇◇◇

**Of course, we said, *Yes.***

# 3

## Classic Chills

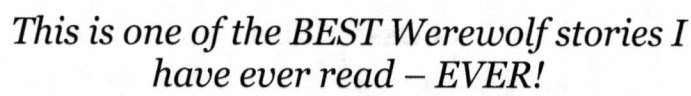

*This is one of the BEST Werewolf stories I have ever read – EVER!*

Lyn Murray

# The White Wolf

## (Written in 1839)

### *Lightly Edited*

### by

# Captain Frederick Marryat

## Captain Frederick Marryat

(10 July 1792 – 9 August 1848)

was a British Royal Navy officer, novelist, and an acquaintance of Charles Dickens, noted today as an early pioneer of the sea story. He is now known particularly for the semi-autobiographical novel *Mr. Midshipman Easy* and his children's novel *The Children of the New Forest*, and for a widely used system of maritime flag signaling, known as Marryat's Code.

Marryat was born in London, the son of Joseph Marryat, a "merchant prince" and member of Parliament and his American wife Charlotte, née von Geyer. After trying to run away to sea several times, he was permitted to enter the Royal Navy in 1806, as a midshipman on board *HMS Imperious*, a frigate commanded by Lord Cochrane (who would later serve as inspiration for both Marryat and other authors).

From 1832 to 1835, Marryat edited *The Metropolitan Magazine*. He kept producing novels, with his biggest success, *Mr. Midshipman Easy*, coming in 1836. He lived in Brussels for a year, travelled in Canada and the United States, then moved to London in 1839, where he was in the literary circle of Charles Dickens and others. He was in North

America in 1837 when the Rebellion of that year in Lower Canada broke out, and served with the British forces in suppressing it.

He was named a Fellow of the Royal Society in recognition of his invention and other achievements. In 1843, he moved to a small farm at Manor Cottage in Norfolk, where he died in 1848. His daughter Florence Marryat later became well known as a writer and actress. His son Francis Samuel Marryat completed his late novel *The Little Savage*.

Marryat's novels are characteristic of their time, with the concerns of family connections and social status often overshadowing the naval action, but they are interesting as fictional renditions of the author's 25 years of real-life experience at sea. These novels, much admired by men like Mark Twain, Joseph Conrad, and Ernest Hemingway, were among the first sea novels. They were models for later works by C. S. Forester and Patrick O'Brian that were also set in the time of Nelson and told the stories of young men rising through the ranks through successes as naval officers. Along with his novels, Marryat was also known for his short writings on nautical subjects. These short stories, plays, pieces of travel journalism and essays appeared in *The Metropolitan Magazine* too, and were later published in book form as *Olla Podrida*.

Marryat's 1839 Gothic novel *The Phantom Ship* contained *The White Wolf of the Hartz Mountains*, which includes the first female werewolf in a short story.

Controversy existed amongst the readers of Marryat's work; as some criticized that he wrote with carelessness. However, others admired the way he wrote about his real life experiences at sea with vivacity.

His later novels were generally for the children's market, including his most famous novel for contemporary readers, *The Children of the New Forest*, which was published in 1847 and set in the countryside surrounding the village of Sway, Hampshire.

## Prologue

(Remember, this story was written in 1839. It is not as fast paced as our modern literature – but oh, so worth the effort, with many twists and turns, plots within plots. Simply delicious! So, if you're ready, this is where I would say – *"Let me set the stage . . ."*)

Scarcely had the soldiers performed their task, and thrown down their shovels, when they commenced an altercation. It appeared that this money was to be again the cause of slaughter and bloodshed. Philip and Krantz determined to sail immediately in one of the peroquas, and leave them to settle their disputes as they pleased. He asked permission of the soldiers to take from the provisions and water, of which there was ample supply, a larger proportion than was their share; stating, that he and Krantz had a long voyage and would require it, and pointing out to them that there were plenty of cocoa-nuts for their support. The soldiers, who thought of nothing but their newly-acquired wealth, allowed him to do as he pleased; and, having hastily collected as many cocoa-nuts as they could, to add to their stock of provisions, before noon, Philip and Krantz had embarked and made sail in the peroqua, leaving the soldiers with their knives again drawn, and so busy in their angry altercation as to be heedless of their departure.

"There will be the same scene over again, I expect," observed Krantz, as the vessel parted swiftly from the shore.

"I have little doubt of it; observe, even now they are at blows and stabs."

"If I were to name that spot, it should be the 'Accursed Isle.'"

"Would not any other be the same, with so much to inflame the passions of men?"

"Assuredly: what a curse is gold!"

"And what a blessing!" replied Krantz. "I am sorry Pedro is left with them."

"It is their destiny," replied Philip; "so let's think no more of them. Now what do you propose? With this vessel, small as she is, we may sail over these seas in safety, and we have, I imagine, provisions sufficient for more than a month."

"My idea is, to run into the track of the vessels going to the westward, and obtain a passage to Goa."

"And if we do not meet with any, we can, at all events, proceed up the Straits, as far as Pulo

Penang without risk. There we may safely remain until a vessel passes."

"I agree with you; it is our best, nay our only, place; unless, indeed, we were to proceed to Cochin, where junks are always leaving for Goa."

"But that would be out of our way, and the junks cannot well pass us in the Straits, without their being seen by us."

They had no difficulty in steering their course; the islands by day, and the clear stars by night, were their compass. It is true that they did not follow the more direct track, but they followed the more secure, working up the smooth waters, and gaining to the northward more than to the west. Many times, they were chased by the Malay proas, which infested the islands, but the swiftness of their little peroqua was their security; indeed, the chase was, generally speaking, abandoned as soon as the smallness of the vessel was made out by the pirates, who expected that little or no booty was to be gained.

That Amine and Philip's mission was the constant theme of their discourse, may easily be imagined. One morning, as they were sailing between the isles, with less wind than usual, Philip observed:

"Krantz, you said that there were events in your own life, or connected with it, which would corroborate the mysterious tale I confided to you. Will you now tell me to what you referred?"

"Certainly," replied Krantz; "I've often thought of doing so, but one circumstance or another has hitherto prevented me; this is, however, a fitting opportunity. Prepare, therefore, to listen to a strange story, quite as strange, perhaps, as your own:--

"I take it for granted, that you have heard people speak of the Hartz Mountains," observed Krantz.

"I have never heard people speak of them, that I can recollect," replied Philip";but I have read of them in some book, and of the strange things which have occurred there."

"It is indeed a wild region," rejoined Krantz, "and many strange tales are told of it; but strange as they are, I have good reason for believing them to be true. I have told you, Philip, that I fully believe in your communion with the other world---that I credit the history of your father, and the lawfulness of your mission; for that we are surrounded, impelled, and worked upon by beings different in their nature from ourselves, I have had full evidence, as you will acknowledge, when I state what has occurred in my own family. Why such malevolent beings as I am about to speak of, should be permitted to interfere with us, and punish, I may say, comparatively unoffending mortals, is beyond my comprehension; but that they are so permitted is most certain."

"The great principle of all evil fulfills his work of evil; why, then, not the other minor spirits of the same class?" inquired Philip. "What matters it to us, whether we are tried by, and have to suffer from, the enmity of our fellow-mortals, or whether we are persecuted by beings more powerful and more malevolent than ourselves? We know that we have to work out our salvation, and that we shall be judged according to our strength; if then there be evil spirits who delight to oppress man, there surely must be, as Amine asserts, good spirits, whose delight is to do him service. Whether, then, we have to struggle against our passions only, or whether we have to struggle not only against our passions, but also the dire influence of unseen enemies, we ever struggle with the same odds in our favor, as the good are stronger than the evil which we combat. In either case, we are on the 'vantage ground, whether, as in the first, we fight the good cause single-handed, or as in the second, although opposed, we have the host of Heaven ranged on our side. Thus are the scales of

Divine justice evenly balanced, and man is still a free agent, as his own virtuous or vicious propensities must ever decide whether he shall gain or lose the victory."

"Most true," replied Krantz, "and now to my history:--

"My father was not born, or originally a resident, in the Hartz Mountains; he was the serf of a Hungarian nobleman, of great possessions, in Transylvania; but, although a serf, he was not by any means a poor or illiterate man. In fact, he was rich and his intelligence and respectability were such, that he had been raised by his lord to the stewardship; but, whoever may happen to be born a serf, a serf must he remain, even though he become a wealthy man: and such was the condition of my father. My father had been married for about five years; and by his marriage had three children---my eldest brother Caesar, a sister and myself (Hermann), named Marcella. You know, Philip, which Latin is still the language spoken in that country; and that will account for our high-sounding names. My mother was a very beautiful woman, unfortunately more beautiful than virtuous: she was seen and admired by the lord of the soil; my father was sent away upon some mission; and, during his absence, my mother, flattered by the attentions, and won by the assiduities (relentless & consistent effort to persuade another), of this nobleman, yielded to his wishes. It so happened that my father returned very unexpectedly, and discovered the intrigue. The evidence of my mother's shame was positive; he surprised her in the company of her seducer! Carried away by the impetuosity of his feelings, he watched the opportunity of a meeting taking place between them, and murdered both his wife and her seducer. Conscious that, as a serf, not even the provocation which he had received would be allowed as a justification of his conduct, he hastily collected together what money he could lay his hands upon, and, as we were then in the depth of winter, he put his horses to the sleigh, and taking his children with him, he set off in the middle of the night, and was far away before the tragically circumstance had transpired. Aware that he would be pursued, and that he had no chance of escape if he remained in any portion of his native country (in which the authorities could lay hold of him), he continued his flight without intermission until he had buried himself in the intricacies and seclusion of the Hartz Mountains. Of course, all that I have now told you I learned afterwards. My oldest recollections are knit to a rude, yet comfortable cottage, in which I lived with my father, brother, and sister. It was on the confines of one of those vast forests, which cover the northern part of Germany; around it were a few acres of ground, which, during the summer months, my father cultivated, and which, though they yielded a doubtful harvest, were sufficient for our support. In the winter, we remained much indoors, for, as my father followed the chase, we were left alone, and the wolves, during that season, incessantly prowled about. My father had purchased the cottage, and land about it, of one of the rude foresters, who gain their livelihood partly by hunting, and partly by burning charcoal, for the purpose of smelting the ore from the neighboring mines; it was distant about two miles from any other habitation. I can call to mind the whole landscape now: the tall pines, which rose up on the mountain above us, and the wide expanse of forest beneath, on the topmost boughs and heads of whose trees we looked down from our cottage, as the mountain below us rapidly descended into the distant valley. In summer time, the prospect was beautiful: but during the severe winter, a more desolate scene could not well be imagined.

"I said that, in the winter, my father occupied himself with the chase; every day he left us, and often would he lock the door, that we might not leave the cottage. He had no one to assist him, or to take care of us---indeed, it was not easy to find a female servant who would live in such a solitude; but could he have found one, my father would nut have received her, for he had imbibed a horror of the sex, as the difference of his conduct towards us, his two boys, and my poor little sister, Marcella evidently proved. You may suppose we were sadly neglected; indeed, we suffered much, for my father, fearful that we might come to some harm, would not allow us fuel, when he left the cottage; and we were obliged, therefore, to creep under the heaps of bears' skins, and there to keep ourselves as warm as we could until he returned in the evening, when a blazing fire was our delight. That my father chose this restless sort of life may appear strange, but the fact was, that he could not remain quiet; whether from the remorse for having committed murder, or from the misery consequent on his change of situation, or from both combined, he was never happy unless he was in a state of activity. Children, however, when left much to themselves, acquire thoughtfulness not common to their age. So it was with us; and during the short cold days of winter, we would sit silent, longing for the happy hours when the snow would melt and the leaves would burst out, and the birds begin their songs, and when we should again be set at liberty.

"Such was our peculiar and savage sort of life until my brother Caesar was nine, myself seven, and my sister five years old, when the circumstances occurred on which is based the extraordinary narrative which I am about to relate.

▼

And now – The White Wolf . . .

# The White Wolf

## A Tale of Hartz Mountains

"One evening my father returned home rather later than usual; he had been unsuccessful, and, as the weather was very severe, and many feet of snow were upon the ground, he was not only very cold, but in a very bad humor. He had brought in wood, and we were all three gladly assisting each other in blowing on the embers to create the blaze, when he caught poor little Marcella by the arm and threw her aside; the child fell, struck her mouth, and bled very much. My brother ran to raise her up. Accustomed to ill-usage and afraid of my father, she did not dare to cry, but looked up in his face very piteously. My father drew his stool nearer to the hearth, muttered something in abuse of women, and busied himself with the fire, which both my brother and I had deserted when our sister was so unkindly treated. A cheerful blaze was soon the result of his exertions; but we did not, as usual, crowd round it. Marcella, still bleeding, retired to a corner, and my brother and I took our seats beside her, while my father hung over the fire gloomily and alone. Such had been our position for about half an hour, when the howl of a wolf, close under the window of the cottage, fell on our ears. My father started up, and seized his gun: the howl was repeated; he examined the priming, and then hastily left the cottage, shutting the door after him. We all waited (anxiously listening), for we thought that if he succeeded in shooting the wolf, he would return in a better humor; and, although he was harsh to all of us, and particularly so to our little sister, still we loved our father, and loved to see him cheerful and happy, for what else had we to look up to? And I may here observe, that perhaps there never were three children who were fonder of each other; we did not, like other children, fight and dispute together; and if, by chance, any disagreement did arise between my elder brother and me, little Marcella would run to us, and kissing us both, seal, through her entreaties, the peace between us. Marcella was a lovely, amiable child; I can recall her beautiful features even now---Alas! poor little Marcella."

"She is dead, then?" observed Philip.

"Dead! Yes, dead!---but how did she die?--- But I must not anticipate, Philip; let me tell my story.

"We waited for some time, but the report of the gun did not reach us, and my elder brother then said, 'Our father has followed the wolf, and will not be back for some time. Marcella, let us wash the blood from your mouth, and then we will leave this corner, and go to the fire and warm ourselves.'

"We did so, and remained there until near midnight, every minute wondering, as it grew later, why our father did not return. We had no idea that he was in any danger, but we thought that he must have chased the wolf for a very long time. 'I will look out and see if father is coming,' said my brother Caesar, going to the door. 'Take care,' said Marcella, 'the wolves must be about now, and we cannot kill them, brother.' My brother opened the door very cautiously, and but a few inches: he peeped out.---'I see nothing,' said he, after a time, and once more, he joined us at the fire. 'We have had no supper,' said I, for my father usually cooked the meat as soon as he came home; and during his absence, we had nothing but the fragments of the preceding day.

"'And if our father comes home after his hunt, Caesar,' said Marcella, 'he will be pleased to have some supper; let us cook it for him and for ourselves.' Caesar climbed upon the stool, and reached down some meat---I forget now whether it was venison or bear's meat; but we cut off the usual quantity, and proceeded to dress it, as we used to do under our father's superintendence. We were all busy putting it into the platters before the fire, to await his coming, when we heard the sound of a horn. We listened---there was a noise outside, and a minute afterwards, my father entered, ushering in a young female, and a large dark man in a hunter's dress.

"Perhaps I had better now relate what was only known to me many years afterwards. When my father had left the cottage, he perceived a large white wolf about thirty yards from him; as soon as the animal saw my father, it retreated slowly, growling and snarling. My father followed; the animal did not run, but always kept at some distance; and my father did not like to fire until he was pretty certain that his ball would take effect; thus they went on for some time, the wolf now leaving my father far behind, and then stopping and snarling defiance at him, and then, again, on his approach, setting off at speed.

"Anxious to shoot the animal (for the white wolf is very rare) my father continued the pursuit for several hours, during which he continually ascended the mountain.

"You must know, Philip, that there are peculiar spots on those mountains which are supposed, and, as my story will prove, truly supposed, to be inhabited by the evil influences: they are well known to the huntsmen, who invariably avoid them. Now, one of these spots, an open space in the pine forests above us, had been pointed out to my father as dangerous on that account. But, whether he disbelieved these wild stories, or whether, in his eager pursuit of the chase, he disregarded them, I know not; certain, however, it is, that he was decoyed by the white wolf to this open space, when the animal appeared to slacken her speed. My father approached, came close up to her, raised his gun to his shoulder, and was about to fire, when the wolf suddenly disappeared. He thought that the snow on the ground must have dazzled his sight, and he let down his gun to look for the beast---but she was gone; how she could have escaped over the clearance, without his seeing her, was beyond his comprehension. Mortified at the ill success of his chase, he was about to retrace his steps, when he heard the distant sound of a horn. Astonishment at such a sound---at such an hour---in such a wilderness, made him forget for the moment his disappointment, and he remained riveted to the spot. In a minute, the horn was blown a second time, and at no great distance; my father stood still, and listened: a third time it was blown. I forget the term used to express it, but it was the signal, which, my father well knew, implied that the party was lost in the woods. In a few minutes more my father beheld a man on horseback, with a female seated on the crupper, enter the cleared space, and ride up to him. At first, my father called to mind the strange stories which

he had heard of the supernatural beings that were said to frequent these mountains; but the nearer approach of the parties satisfied him that they were mortals like himself. As soon as they came up to him, the man who guided the horse accosted him. 'Friend Hunter, you are out late, the better fortune for us; we have ridden far, and are in fear of our lives which are eagerly sought after. These mountains have enabled us to elude our pursuers; but if we find not shelter and refreshment, that will avail us little, as we must perish from hunger and the inclemency of the night. My daughter, who rides behind me, is now more dead than alive---say, can you assist us in our difficulty?'

"'My cottage is some few miles distant,' replied my father, 'but I have little to offer you besides a shelter from the weather; to the little I have you are welcome. May I ask whence you come?'

"'Yes, friend, it is no secret now; we have escaped from Transylvania, where my daughter's honor and my life were equally in jeopardy!'

"This information was quite enough to raise an interest in my father's heart, he remembered his own escape; he remembered the loss of his wife's honor, and the tragedy by which it was wound up. He immediately, and warmly, offered all the assistance, which he could afford them.

"'There is no time to be lost then, good sir,' observed the horseman; 'my daughter is chilled with the frost, and cannot hold out much longer against the severity of the weather.'

"'Follow me,' replied my father, leading the way towards his home.

"'I was lured away in pursuit of a large white wolf,' observed my father; 'it came to the very window of my hut, or I should not have been out at this time of night.'

"'The creature passed by us just as we came out of the wood,' said the female, in a silvery tone.

"'I was nearly discharging my piece at it,' observed the hunter; 'but since it did us such good service, I am glad I allowed it to escape.'

"In about an hour and a half, during which my father walked at a rapid pace, the party arrived at the cottage, and, as I said before, came in.

"'We are in good time, apparently,' observed the dark hunter, catching the smell of the roasted meat, as he walked to the fire and surveyed my brother and sister, and myself.'You have young cooks here, Meinheer.' 'I am glad that we shall not have to wait,' replied my father. 'Come, mistress, seat yourself by the fire; you require warmth after your cold ride.' 'And where can I put up my horse, Meinheer?' observed the huntsman. 'I will take care of him,' replied my father, going out of the cottage door.

"The female must, however, be particularly described. She was young, and apparently twenty years of age. She was dressed in a travelling-dress, deeply bordered with white fur, and wore a cap of white ermine on her head. Her features were very beautiful, at least I thought so, and so my father has since declared. Her hair was flaxen, glossy, and shining, and bright as a mirror; and her

mouth, although somewhat large when it was open, showed the most brilliant teeth I have ever beheld. But there was something about her eyes, bright as they were, which made us children afraid; they were so restless, so furtive; I could not at that time tell why, but I felt as if there was cruelty in her eye; and when she beckoned us to come to her, we approached her with fear and trembling. Still she was beautiful, very beautiful. She spoke kindly to my brother and myself, patted our heads, and caressed us; but Marcella would not come near her; on the contrary, she slunk away, and hid herself in the bed, and would not wait for the supper, which half an hour before she had been so anxious for.

"My father, having put the horse into a close shed, soon returned, and supper was placed upon the table. When it was over, my father requested that the young lady would take possession of his bed, and he would remain at the fire, and sit up with her father. After some hesitation on her part, this arrangement was agreed to, and my brother and I crept into the other bed with Marcella, for we had as yet always slept together.

"But we could not sleep; there was something so unusual, not only in seeing strange people, but in having those people sleep at the cottage, that we were bewildered. As for poor little Marcella, she was quiet, but I perceived that she trembled during the whole night, and sometimes I thought that she was checking a sob. My father had brought out some spirits, which he rarely used, and he and the strange hunter remained drinking and talking before the fire. Our ears were ready to catch the slightest whisper---so much was our curiosity excited.

"'You said you came from Transylvania?' observed my father.

"'Even so, Meinheer,' replied the hunter.'I was a serf to the noble house of---; my master would insist upon my surrendering up my fair girl to his wishes: it ended in my giving him a few inches of my hunting-knife.'

"'We are countrymen, and brothers in misfortune,' replied my father, taking the huntsman's hand, and pressing it warmly.

"'Indeed! Are you then from that country?'

"'Yes, and I too have fled for my life. But mine is a melancholy tale.'

"'Your name?' inquired the hunter.

"'Krantz.'

"'What! Krantz of---? I have heard your tale; you need not renew your grief by repeating it now. Welcome, most welcome, Meinheer, and, I may say, my worthy kinsman. I am your second cousin, Wilfred of Barnsdorf,' cried the hunter, rising up and embracing my father.

"They filled their horn-mugs to the brim, and drank to one another after the German fashion. The conversation was then carried on in a low tone; all that we could collect from it was that our new relative and his daughter were to take up their abode in our cottage, at least for the present. In about an hour, they both fell back in their chairs and appeared to sleep.

"'Marcella, dear, did you hear?' said my brother, in a low tone.

"'Yes,' replied Marcella in a whisper, 'I heard all. Oh! Brother, I cannot bear to look upon that woman---I feel so frightened.'

"My brother made no reply, and shortly afterwards we were all three fast asleep.

"When we awoke the next morning, we found that the hunter's daughter had risen before us. I thought she looked more beautiful than ever. She came up to little Marcella and caressed her: the child burst into tears, and sobbed as if her heart would break.

"But, not to detain you with too long a story, the huntsman and his daughter were accommodated in the cottage. My father and he went out hunting daily, leaving Christina with us. She performed all the household duties; was very kind to us children; and, gradually, the dislike even of little Marcella wore away. But a great change took place in my father; he appeared to have conquered his aversion to the sex, and was most attentive to Christina. Often, after her father and we were in bed would he sit up with her, conversing in a low tone by the fire. I ought to have mentioned that my father and the huntsman Wilfred, slept in another portion of the cottage, and that the bed which he formerly occupied, and which was in the same room as ours, had been given up to the use of Christina. These visitors had been about three weeks at the cottage, when, one night, after we children had been sent to bed, a consultation was held. My father had asked Christina in marriage, and had obtained both her own consent and that of Wilfred; after this, a conversation took place, which was, as nearly as I can recollect, as follows.

"'You may take my child, Meinheer Krantz, and my blessing with her, and I shall then leave you and seek some other habitation---it matters little where.'

"'Why not remain here, Wilfred?'

"'No, no, I am called elsewhere; let that suffice, and ask no more questions. You have my child.'

"'I thank you for her, and will duly value her; but there is one difficulty.'

"'I know what you would say; there is no priest here in this wild country: true; neither is there any law to bind; still must some ceremony pass between you, to satisfy a father. Will you consent to marry her after my fashion? if so, I will marry you directly.'

"'I will,' replied my father.

"'Then take her by the hand. Now, Meinheer, swear.'

"'I swear,' repeated my father.

"'By all the spirits of the Hartz mountains--'

"'Nay, why not by Heaven?' interrupted my father.

"'Because it is not my humor,' rejoined Wilfred; 'if I prefer that oath, less binding perhaps, than another, surely you will not thwart me.'

"'Well be it so then; have your humor. Will you make me swear by that in which I do not believe?'

"'Yet many do so, who in outward appearance are Christians,' rejoined Wilfred; 'say, will you be married, or shall I take my daughter away with me?'

"'Proceed,' replied my father, impatiently.

"'I swear by all the spirits of the Hartz mountains, by all their power for good or for evil, that I take Christina for my wedded wife; that I will ever protect her, cherish her, and love her; that my hand shall never be raised against her to harm her.'

"My father repeated the words after Wilfred.

"'And if I fail in this my vow, may all the vengeance of the spirits fall upon me and upon my children; may they perish by the vulture, by the wolf, or other beasts of the forest; may their flesh be torn from their limbs, and their bones blanch in the wilderness: all this I swear.'

"My father hesitated, as he repeated the last words; little Marcella could not restrain herself, and as my father repeated the last sentence, she burst into tears. This sudden interruption appeared to discompose the party, particularly my father; he spoke harshly to the child, who controlled her sobs, burying her face under the bedclothes.

"Such was the second marriage of my father. The next morning, the hunter Wilfred mounted his horse, and rode away.

"My father resumed his bed, which was in the same room as ours; and things went on much as before the marriage, except that our new mother-in-law did not show any kindness towards us; indeed during my father's absence, she would often beat us, particularly little Marcella, and her eyes would flash fire, as she looked eagerly upon the fair and lovely child.

"One night, my sister awoke me and my brother.

"'What is the matter?' said Caesar.

"'She has gone out,' whispered Marcella.

"'Gone out!'

"'Yes, gone out at the door, in her night-clothes,' replied the child; 'I saw her get out of bed, look at my father to see if he slept, and then she went out at the door.'

"What could induce her to leave her bed, and all undressed to go out, in such bitter wintry weather, with the snow deep on the ground was to us incomprehensible; we lay awake, and in about an hour we heard the growl of a wolf, close under the window.

"'There is a wolf,' said Caesar. 'She will be torn to pieces.'

"'Oh no!' cried Marcella.

"In a few minutes afterwards our mother-in-law appeared; she was in her night-dress, as Marcella had stated. She let down the latch of the door, so as to make no noise, went to a pail of water, and washed her face and hands, and then slipped into the bed where my father lay.

"We all three trembled---we hardly knew why; but we resolved to watch the next night: we did so; and not only on the ensuing night, but on many others, and always at about the same hour, would our mother-in-law rise from her bed and leave the cottage; and after she was gone we invariably heard the growl of a wolf under our window, and always saw her, on her return, wash herself before she retired to bed. We observed also that she seldom sat down to meals, and that when she did she appeared to eat with dislike; but when the meat was taken down to be prepared for dinner, she would often furtively (slyly) put a raw piece into her mouth.

"My brother Caesar was a courageous boy; he did not like to speak to my father until he knew more. He resolved that he would follow her out, and ascertain what she did. Marcella and I endeavored to dissuade him from this project; but he would not be controlled; and the very next night he lay down in his clothes, and as soon as our mother-in-law had left the cottage, he jumped up, took down my father's gun, and followed her.

"You may imagine in what a state of suspense Marcella and I remained during his absence. After a few minutes, we heard the report of a gun. It did not awaken my father; and we lay trembling with anxiety. In a minute afterwards, we saw our mother-in-law enter the cottage---her dress was bloody. I put my hand to Marcella's mouth to prevent her crying out, although I was myself in great alarm. Our mother-in-law approached my father's bed, looked to see if he was asleep, and then went to the chimney and blew up the embers into a blaze.

"'Who is there?' said my father, waking up.

"'Lie still, dearest,' replied my mother-in-law; 'it is only me; I have lighted the fire to warm some water; I am not quite well.'

"My father turned round, and was soon asleep; but we watched our mother-in-law. She changed her linen, and threw the garments she had worn into the fire; and we then perceived that her right leg was bleeding profusely, as if from a gunshot wound. She bandaged it up, and then dressing herself, remained before the fire until the break of day.

"Poor little Marcella, her heart beat quick as she pressed me to her side---so indeed did mine. Where was our brother Caesar? How did my mother-in-law receive the wound unless from his gun? At last my father rose, and then for the first time I spoke, saying, 'Father, where is my brother Caesar?'

"'Your brother!' exclaimed he; 'why, where can he be?'

"'Merciful Heaven! I thought, as lay very restless last night,' observed our mother-in-law, 'that I heard somebody open the latch of the door; and, dear me, husband, what has become of your gun?'

"My father cast his eyes up above the chimney, and perceived that his gun was missing. For a moment he looked perplexed; then, seizing a broad axe, he went out of the cottage without saying another word.

"He did not remain away from us long; in a few minutes he returned, bearing in his arms the mangled body of my poor brother; he laid it down, and covered up his face.

"My mother-in-law rose up, and looked at the body, while Marcella and I threw ourselves by its side, wailing and sobbing bitterly.

"'Go to bed again, children,' said she, sharply.'Husband,' continued she, 'your boy must have taken the gun down, to shoot a wolf, and the animal has been too powerful for him. Poor boy! he has paid dearly for his rashness.'

"My father made no reply. I wished to speak--- to tell all---but Marcella who perceived my intention, held me by the arm, and looked at me so imploringly, that I desisted (ceased).

"My father, therefore, was left in his error; but Marcella and I, although we could not comprehend it, were conscious that our mother-in-law was in some way connected with my brother's death.

"That day my father went out and dug a grave; and when he hid the body in the earth, he piled up stones over it so that the wolves should not be able to dig it up. The shock of this catastrophe was to my poor father very severe; for several days he never went to the chase, although at times he would utter bitter anathemas (curses) and vengeance against the wolves.

"But during this time of mourning on his part, my mother-in-law's nocturnal wanderings continued with the same regularity as before.

"At last my father took down his gun to repair to the forest; but he soon returned, and appeared much annoyed.

"'Would you believe it, Christina, that the wolves---perdition to the whole race---have actually contrived to dig up the body of my poor boy, and now there is nothing left of him but his bones?'

"'Indeed!' replied my mother-in-law. Marcella looked at me; and I saw in her intelligent eye all she would have uttered.

"'A wolf growls under our window every night, father,' said I.

"'Ay, indeed! Why did you not tell me, boy? Wake me the next time you hear it.'

"I saw my mother-in-law turn away; her eyes flashed fire, and she gnashed her teeth.

"My father went out again, and covered up with a larger pile of stones the little remnants of my poor brother which the wolves had spared. Such was the first act of the tragedy.

"The spring now came on; the snow disappeared, and we were permitted to leave the cottage; but never would I quit for one moment my dear little sister, to whom since the death of my brother, I was more ardently attached than ever; indeed, I was afraid to leave her alone with my mother-in-law, who appeared to have a particular pleasure in ill-treating the child. My father was now employed upon his little farm, and I was able to render him some assistance.

"Marcella used to sit by us while we were at work, leaving my mother-in-law alone in the cottage. I ought to observe that, as the spring advanced, so did my mother-in-law decrease her nocturnal rambles, and that we never heard the growl of the wolf under the window after I had spoken of it to my father.

"One day, when my father and I were in the field, Marcella being with us, my mother-in-law came out, saying that she was going into the forest to collect some herbs my father wanted, and that Marcella must go to the cottage and watch the dinner. Marcella went; and my mother-in-law soon disappeared in the forest, taking a direction quite contrary to that in which the cottage stood, and leaving my father and me, as it were, between her and Marcella.

"About an hour afterwards we were startled by shrieks from the cottage---evidently the shrieks of little Marcella.'Marcella has burnt herself, father,' said I, throwing down my spade. My father threw down his, and we both hastened to the cottage. Before we could gain the door, out darted a large white wolf, which fled with the utmost celerity (swift urgency). My father had no weapon; he rushed into the cottage, and there saw poor little Marcella expiring. Her body was dreadfully mangled, and the blood pouring from it had formed a large pool on the cottage floor. My father's first intention had been to seize his gun and pursue; but he was checked by this horrid spectacle; he knelt down by his dying child, and burst into tears. Marcella could just look kindly on us for a few seconds, and then her eyes were closed in death.

"My father and I were still hanging over my poor sister's body, when my mother-in-law came in. At the dreadful sight, she expressed much concern; but she did not appear to recoil from the sight of blood, as most women do.

"'Poor child!' said she, 'it must have been that great white wolf which passed me just now, and frightened me so. She's quite dead, Krantz.'

"'I know it---I know it!' cried my father, in agony.

"I thought my father would never recover from the effects of this second tragedy; he mourned bitterly over the body of his sweet child, and for several days would not consign it to its grave, although frequently requested by my mother-in-law to do so. At last, he yielded, and dug a grave for her close by that of my poor brother, and took every precaution that the wolves should not violate her remains.

"I was now really miserable, as I lay alone in the bed which I had formerly shared with my brother and sister. I could not help thinking that my mother-in-law was implicated in both their deaths, although I could not account for the manner; but I no longer felt afraid of her; my little heart was full of hatred and revenge.

"The night after my sister had been buried, as I lay awake, I perceived my mother-in-law get up and go out of the cottage. I waited some time, then dressed myself, and looked out through the door, which I half opened. The moon shone bright and I could see the spot where my brother and my sister had been buried; and what was my horror when I perceived my mother-in-law busily removing the stones from Marcella's grave!

"She was in her white night-dress and the moon shone full upon her. She was digging with her hands, and throwing away the stones behind her with all the ferocity of a wild beast. It was some time before I could collect my senses, and decide what I should do. At last, I perceived that she had arrived at the body, and raised it up to the side of the grave. I could bear it no longer; I ran to my father and awoke him.

"'Father, father!' cried I, 'dress yourself, and get your gun.'

"'What!' cried my father, 'the wolves are there, are they?'

"He jumped out of bed, threw on his clothes, and, in his anxiety, did not appear to perceive the absence of his wife. As soon as he was ready, I opened the door; he went out, and I followed him.

"Imagine his horror, when (unprepared as he was for such a sight) he beheld, as he advanced towards the grave not a wolf, but his wife, in her night-dress, on her hands and knees, crouching by the body of my sister, and tearing off large pieces of the flesh, and devouring them with all the avidity (greed) of a wolf. She was too busy to be aware of our approach. My father dropped his gun; his hair stood on end, so did mine; he breathed heavily, and then his breath for a time stopped. I picked up the gun and put it into his hand. Suddenly he appeared as if concentrated rage had restored him to double vigor; he leveled his piece, fired, and with a loud shriek down fell the wretch whom he had fostered in his bosom.

"'God of Heaven!' cried my father, sinking down upon the earth in a swoon, as soon as he had discharged his gun.

"I remained some time by his side before he recovered. 'Where am I?' said he, 'what has happened? Oh!---yes, yes! I recollect now. Heaven forgive me!'

"He rose and we walked up to the grave; what again was our astonishment and horror to find that, instead of the dead body of my mother-in-law, as we expected, there was lying over the remains of my poor sister, a large white she-wolf.

"'The white wolf!' exclaimed my father, 'the white wolf which decoyed me into the forest---I see it all now---I have dealt with the spirits of the Hartz Mountains.'

"For some time my father remained in silence and deep thought. He then carefully lifted up the body of my sister, replaced it in the grave, and covered it over as before, having struck the head of the dead animal with the heel of his boot, and raving like a madman. He walked back to the cottage, shut the door, and threw himself on the bed; I did the same, for I was in a stupor of amazement.

"Early in the morning we were both roused by a loud knocking at the door, and in rushed the hunter Wilfred.

"'My daughter---man---my daughter!---where is my daughter?' cried he in a rage.

"'Where the wretch, the fiend, should be, I trust,' replied my father, starting up, and displaying equal choler; 'where she should be---in hell! Leave this cottage, or you may fare worse.'

"'Ha---ha!' replied the hunter, 'would you harm a potent spirit of the Hartz Mountains.

Poor mortal, whom out of need – wed a werewolf.'

"'Out, demon! I defy thee and thy power.'

"'Yet shall you feel it; remember your oath--- your solemn oath---never to raise your hand against her to harm her.'

"'I made no pact with evil spirits.'

"'You did, and if you failed in your vow, you were to meet the vengeance of the spirits. Your children were to perish by the vulture, the wolf--'

"'Out, out, demon!'

"'And their bones blanch in the wilderness. Ha!---ha!'

"My father, frantic with rage, seized his axe, and raised it over Wilfred's head to strike.

"'All this I swear,' continued the huntsman, mockingly.

"The axe descended; but it passed through the form of the hunter, and my father lost his balance, and fell heavily on the floor.

"'Mortal!' said the hunter, striding over my father's body, 'we have power over those only who have committed murder. You have been guilty of a double murder: you shall pay the penalty attached to your marriage vow. Two of your children are gone, the third is yet to follow---and follow them he will, for your oath is registered. Go---it were kindness to kill thee---your punishment is, that you live!'

"With these words the spirit disappeared. My father rose from the floor, embraced me tenderly, and knelt down in prayer.

"The next morning he quitted the cottage for ever. He took me with him, and bent his steps to Holland, where we safely arrived. He had some little money with him; but he had not been many days in Amsterdam before he was seized with a brain fever, and died raving mad. I was put into the asylum, and afterwards was sent to sea before the mast. You now know all my history. The question is, whether I am to pay the penalty of my father's oath? I am myself perfectly convinced that, in some way or another, I shall."

On the twenty-second day the high land of the south of Sumatra was in view: as there were no vessels in sight, they resolved to keep their course through the Straits, and run for Pulo Penang, which they expected, as their vessel lay so close to the wind, to reach in seven or eight days. By constant exposure, Philip and Krantz were now so bronzed that with their long beards and Mussulman dresses, they might easily have passed off for natives. They had steered the whole of the days exposed to a burning sun; they had lain down and slept in the dew of the night; but their health had not suffered. But for several days, since he had confided the history of his family to Philip, Krantz had become silent and melancholy: his usual flow of spirits had vanished and Philip had often questioned him as to the cause. As they entered the Straits, Philip talked of what they should do upon their arrival at Goa; when Krantz gravely replied, "For some days, Philip, I have had a presentiment (foreboding) that I shall never see that city."

"You are out of health, Krantz," replied Philip.

"No, I am in sound health, body, and mind. I have endeavored to shake off the presentiment, but in vain; there is a warning voice that continually tells me that I shall not be long with you. Philip, will you oblige me by making me content on one point? I have gold about my person which may be useful to you; oblige me by taking it, and securing it on your own."

"What nonsense, Krantz."

"It is no nonsense, Philip. Have you not had your warnings? Why should I not have mine? You know that I have little fear in my composition, and that I care not about death; but I feel the presentiment (foreboding) which I speak of more strongly every hour. It is some kind spirit who would warn me to prepare for another world. Be it so. I have lived long enough in this world to leave it without regret; although to part with you and Amine, the only two now dear to me, is painful, I acknowledge."

"May not this arise from over-exertion and fatigue, Krantz? Consider how much excitement you have labored under within these last four months. Is not that enough to create a corresponding depression? Depend upon it, my dear friend, such is the fact."

"I wish it were; but I feel otherwise, and there is a feeling of gladness connected with the idea that I am to leave this world, arising from another presentiment (foreboding feeling), which equally occupies my mind."

"I hardly can tell you---but Amine and you are connected with it. In my dreams I have seen you meet again; but it has appeared to me as if a portion of your trial was purposely shut from my sight in dark clouds; and I have asked, 'May not I see what is there concealed?'---and an invisible has answered, 'No! 'twould make you wretched. Before these trials take place, you will be summoned away:' and then I have thanked Heaven, and felt resigned."

"These are the imaginings of a disturbed brain, Krantz; that I am destined to suffering may be true; but why Amine should suffer, or why you, young, in full health and vigor should not pass your days in peace, and live to a good old age, there is no cause for believing. You will be better tomorrow."

"Perhaps so," replied Krantz; "but still you must yield to my whim, and take the gold. If I am wrong, and we do arrive safe, you know, Philip, you can let me have it back," observed Krantz, with a faint smile---"but you forget, our water is nearly out, and we must look out for a rill on the coast to obtain a fresh supply."

"I was thinking of that when you commenced this unwelcome topic. We had better look out for the water before dark, and as soon as we have replenished our jars, we will make sail again."

At the time that this conversation took place; they were on the eastern side of the strait, about forty miles to the northward. The interior of the coast was rocky and mountainous; but it slowly descended to low land of alternate forest and jungles, which continued to the beach: the country appeared to be uninhabited. Keeping close in to the shore, they discovered, after two hours' run, a fresh stream, which burst in a cascade from the mountains, and swept its devious course through the jungle, until it poured its tribute into the waters of the strait.

They ran close in to the mouth of the stream, lowered the sails, and pulled the peroqua against the current, until they had advanced far enough to assure them that the water was quite fresh. The jars were soon filled, and they were again thinking of pushing off; when, enticed by the beauty of the spot, the coolness of the fresh water, and wearied with their long confinement on board of the peroqua, they proposed to bathe---a luxury hardly to be appreciated by those who have not been in a similar situation. They threw off their Mussulmen dresses, and plunged into the stream, where they remained fur some time. Krantz was the first to get out: he complained of feeling chilled, and he walked on to the banks where their clothes had been laid. Philip also approached nearer to the beach, intending to follow him.

"And now, Philip," said Krantz, "this will be a good opportunity for me to give you the money. I will open my sash and pour it out, and you can put it into your own before you put it on."

Philip was standing in the water, which was about level with his waist.

"Well, Krantz," said he, "I suppose if it must be so, it must---but it appears to me an idea so ridiculous---however, you shall have your own way."

Philip quitted the run, and sat down by Krantz, who was already busy in shaking the doubloons out of the folds of his sash---at last he said--

"I believe, Philip, you have got them all now?---I feel satisfied."

"What danger there can be to you, which I am not equally exposed to, I cannot conceive," replied Philip; "however--"

Hardly had he said these words, when there was a tremendous roar---a rush like a mighty wind through the air---a blow that threw him on his back---a loud cry---and a contention. Philip recovered himself, and perceived the naked form of Krantz carried off with the speed of an arrow by an enormous tiger through the jungle. He watched with distended eyeballs; in a few seconds the animal and Krantz had disappeared!

"God of Heaven! would that thou hadst spared me this," cried Philip, throwing himself down in agony on his face. "Oh! Krantz, my friend---my brother---too sure was your presentiment (sense of foreboding). Merciful God! have pity---but thy will be done;" and Philip burst into a flood of tears.

For more than an hour did he remain fixed upon the spot, careless and indifferent to the danger by which he was surrounded. At last, somewhat recovered, he rose, dressed himself, and then again sat down---his eyes fixed upon the clothes of Krantz, and the gold which still lay on the sand.

"He would give me that gold. He foretold his doom. Yes! yes! It was his destiny, and it has been fulfilled. His bones will bleach in the wilderness, and the spirit-hunter and his wolfish daughter are avenged."

The shades of evening now set in, and the low growling of the beasts of the forest recalled Philip to a sense of his own danger. He thought of Amine; and hastily making the clothes of Krantz and the doubloons into a package, he stepped into the peroqua, with difficulty shoved it off, and with a melancholy heart, and in silence, hoisted the sail, and pursued his course.

"Yes, Amine," thought Philip, as he watched the stars twinkling and coruscating (vivid flashes of light); "yes, you are right, when you assert that the destinies of men are foreknown, and may by some be read. My destiny is, alas! That I should be severed from all I value upon earth, and die friendless and alone. Then welcome death, if such is to be the case; welcome---a thousand welcomes! What a relief wilt thou be to me! What joy to find myself summoned to where the weary are at rest! I have my task to fulfill. God grant that it may soon be accomplished, and let not my life be embittered by any more trials such as this."

Again did Philip weep, for Krantz had been his long-tried, valued friend, his partner in all his dangers and privations (hardships), from the period that they had met when the Dutch fleet attempted the passage round Cape Horn.

After seven days of painful watching and brooding over bitter thoughts, Philip arrived at Pulo Penang, where he found a vessel about to sail for the city to which he was destined. He ran his peroqua alongside of her, and found that she was a brig under the Portuguese flag, having, however, but two Portuguese on board, the rest of the crew being natives. Representing himself as an Englishman in the Portuguese service, who had been wrecked, and offering to pay for his passage, he was willingly received, and in a few days, the vessel sailed.

Their voyage was prosperous; in six weeks, they anchored in the roads of Goa; the next day they went up the river. The Portuguese captain informed Philip where he might obtain lodging; and passing him off as one of his crew, there was no difficulty raised as to his landing. Having located himself at his new lodging, Philip commenced some inquiries of his host relative to Amine, designating her merely as a young woman who had arrived there in a vessel some weeks before, but he could obtain no information concerning her. "Signor," said the host, "tomorrow is the grand auto-da-fe' (penance); we can do nothing until that is over; afterwards, I will put you in the way to find out what you wish. In the mean time, you can walk about the town; tomorrow I will take you to where you can behold the grand procession, and then we will try what we can do to assist you in your search."

Philip went out, procured a suit of clothes, removed his beard, and then walked about the town, looking up at every window to see if he could perceive Amine. At a corner of one of the streets, he thought he recognized Father Mathias, and ran up to him; but the monk had drawn his cowl over his head, and when addressed by that name, made no reply.

"I was deceived," thought Philip"; but I really thought it was him." And Philip was right; it was Father Mathias, who thus screened himself from Philip's recognition.

Tired, at last he returned to his hotel, just before it was dark. The company there was numerous; everybody for miles distant had come to Goa to witness the auto-da-fe' (penance) and everybody was discussing the ceremony.

"I will see this grand procession," said Philip to himself, as he threw himself on his bed. "It will drive thought from me for a time; and God knows how painful my thoughts have now become. Amine, dear Amine, may angels guard thee!"

▼

**THE LYCANTHROPIST**

by Catherine Crowe

(1850)

## Catherine Ann Crowe, née Stevens

September 20, 1803 – June 14, 1876

An English novelist, storywriter, and playwright was born in Borough Green, Kent, and died in Folkestone.

Crowe was educated at home, spending most her childhood in Kent. She married an army officer, Major John Crowe (1783–1860). They had a son, John William (born 1823), but the marriage was an unhappy one, and when she met Sydney Smith and his family at Clifton, Bristol in 1828, she asked them for their help. Little is known about the next few years, but by 1838 she was separated from her husband, living in Edinburgh, and had made the acquaintance of several writers, including the impecunious Thomas de Quincey, and in

London Harriet Martineau and William Makepeace Thackeray. Smith was also an encouragement to her in her writing. Her success waned somewhat in the later 1850s and she sold her copyrights in 1861. After 1852, she lived mainly in London and abroad, but she moved to Folkestone in 1871, where she died the following year.

Crowe's two plays, the verse tragedy *Aristodemus* (1838) and the melodrama *The Cruel Kindness* (1853) both had historical themes paralleling her own family problems. Both were published and the second also had a short run in London in 1853.

The book that established Crowe as a novelist was *The Adventures of Susan Hopley* (1841). Men and Women (1844), the well-received The Story of Lily Dawson (1847), The Adventures of a Beauty (1852), and Linny Lockwood (1854), followed it. Though set in middle-class life, they had complicated, sensational plots, while also commenting on the predicaments of Victorian women brought up in seclusion to be mistreated by men. Particularly later women writers in an appreciation in Women Novelists of Queen Victoria's Reign (1897) emphasized this aspect of her writing. *Susan Hopley* was reprinted many times, and to her annoyance, dramatized crudely and turned into a penny serial. Her stories were also in demand from periodicals such as the weekly *Chambers' Edinburgh Journal* and Dickens's *Household Words.*

Crowe turned increasingly to supernatural subjects, inspired by German writers. Her collection *The Night-side of Nature* (1848) became her most popular work and was reprinted as recently as 2000. It was translated into German and French, and is said to have influenced the views of Charles Baudelaire. Her own involvement in such matters came to a bizarre culmination in February 1854, when she was discovered naked in Edinburgh one night, convinced that spirits had rendered her invisible. She was treated for mental illness and recovered. Two of her ghost stories reappeared in *Victorian Ghost Stories* (1936), edited by Montague Summers.

Crowe also wrote a number of books for children, including versions of *Uncle Tom's Cabin* for young readers, *Pippie's Warning; or, Mind Your Temper* (1848). *The Story of Arthur Hunter and his First Shilling* (1861) and *The Adventures of a Monkey* (1862).

# THE LYCANTHROPIST
by Catherine Crowe

Whoever has read the "Arabian Nights' Entertainments," will be acquainted with the words, ghoul, and vampyre. A ghoul was believed to be a being in the human form, which frequented graveyards and cemeteries, where it disinterred, tore to pieces, and devoured the bodies buried there. A vampyre was a dead person, who came out of his grave at night to suck the blood of the living, and whoever was so sucked became a vampyre in his turn when he died.

Both these persuasions have been rejected by the modern scientific world as altogether unworthy of credence or inquiry, although, about a century ago, the exploits of vampyres created such a sensation in Hungary, that they reached the ears of Louis XV., who directed his minister at Vienna to report upon them.

In a newspaper of that period, there appeared a paragraph to the effect that Arnold Paul, a native of Madveiga, being crushed to death by a wagon, and buried, had since become a vampyre, and that he had himself been previously bitten by one.

The authorities being informed of the terror

his visits were occasioning, and several persons having died with all the symptoms of vampyrism, his grave was solemnly opened, and, although he had been in it forty days, the body was like that of a living man.

To cure his roving propensities, a stake was driven into it, whereupon he uttered a cry; after which his head was cut off, and the body burnt. Four other bodies, which had died from the consequences of his bites, and which were found in the same perfectly healthy condition, were served in a similar manner; and it was hoped that these vigorous measures would extinguish the mischief.

But no such thing. The evil continued more or less, and, five years afterwards, was so rife, that the authorities determined to make a thorough clearance of these troublesome individuals.

On this occasion a vast number of graves were opened, of persons of all ages and both sexes; and, strange to say, the bodies of all those accused of plaguing the living by their nocturnal visits, were found in the vampyre state—full of blood, and free from every symptom of death.

The documents, which record these transactions, bear the date of June 7, 1732, and are signed and witnessed by three surgeons and other creditable persons. The facts, in short, are indubitable, though what interpretation to put upon them remains extremely difficult.

One that has been suggested is, that all these supposed vampyres were persons who had fallen into a state of catalepsy or trance, and been buried alive. However this may be, the mystery is sufficiently perplexing; and the more so, that through the whole of Eastern Europe innumerable instances of the same kind of thing have occurred, whilst each language has an especial word to designate it.

That which in the East is called 'ghoulism' has in the West been denominated 'lycanthropy,' or 'wolf mania;' and this phenomenon, as well as vampyrism, has been treated of by numerous ancient authors; and though latterly utterly denied and scouted, was once very generally believed.

There are various shades and degrees of lycanthropy. In some cases, the lycanthrope declares that he has the power of transforming himself into a wolf, in which disguise his tastes corresponding to his form—he delights in feeding on human flesh; and in the public examinations of these unhappy individuals, there was no scarcity of witnesses to corroborate their confessions. In other instances, there was no transformation, and the lycanthrope appears more closely to resemble a ghoul.

In the year 1603, a case of lycanthropy was brought before the Parliament of Bordeaux. The person accused was a boy of fourteen, called Jean Grenier, who herded cattle. Several witnesses, chiefly young girls, came forward as his accusers, declaring that he had attacked and wounded them in the disguise of a wolf, and would have killed them but for the vigorous defense they made with sticks. Jean Grenier himself avowed the crime, confessing to having killed and eaten several children; and the father of the children confirmed all he said. Jean Grenier, however, appears to have been little removed from an idiot.

In the fifteenth century, lycanthropy prevailed extensively amongst the Vaudois, and many persons suffered death for it; but as no similar case seems to have been heard of for a long while, lycanthropy and ghoulism were set down amongst the superstitions of the East, and the follies and fables of the dark ages. A circumstance, however, has just now come to light in France that throws a strange and unexpected light upon this curious subject.

The account we are going to give is drawn from a report of the investigation before a council of war, held on the 10th of the present month (July 1849), Colonel Manselon, president. It is remarked that the court was extremely crowded, and that many ladies were present.

The facts of this mysterious affair, as they came to light in the examinations, are as follow: For some months past the cemeteries in and around Paris have been the scenes of a frightful profanation, the authors of which had succeeded in eluding all the vigilance that WAS exerted to detect them. At one time, the guardians or keepers of these places of burial were themselves suspected; at others, the odium was thrown on the surviving relations of the dead.

The cemetery of Pere la Chaise was the first field of these horrible operations. It appears that for a considerable time the guardians had observed a mysterious figure flitting about by night amongst the tombs, on whom they never could lay their hands. As they approached, he disappeared like a phantom; and even the dogs that were let loose, and urged to seize him, stopped short, and ceased to bark, as if they were trans-fixed by a charm. When morning broke, the ravages of this strange visitant were but too visible—graves had been opened, coffins forced, and the remains of the dead, frightfully torn and mutilated, lay scattered upon the earth. Could the surgeons be the guilty parties? No. A member of the profession being brought to the spot, declared that no scientific knife had been there; but certain parts of the human body might be required for anatomical studies, and the gravediggers might have violated the tombs to obtain money by the sale of them. . . . The watch was doubled; but to no purpose.

A young soldier was one night seized in a tomb, but he declared he had gone there to meet his sweetheart, and had fallen asleep; and as he evinced no trepidation, they let him go.

At length these profanations ceased in Pere la Chaise, but it was not long before they were renewed in another quarter. A suburban cemetery was the new theatre of operations. A little girl aged seven years, and much loved by her parents, died. With their own hands they laid her in her coffin, attired in the frock she delighted to wear on fete days, and with her favorite playthings beside her and accompanied by numerous relatives and friends, they saw her laid in the earth. On the following morning it was discovered that the grave had been violated, the body torn from the coffin, frightfully mutilated, and the heart extracted. There was no robbery: the sensation in the neighborhood was tremendous; and in the general terror and perplexity, suspicion fell on the broken-hearted father, whose innocence, however, was easily proved. Every means were taken to discover the criminal; but the only result of the increased surveillance was, that the scene of profanation was removed to the cemetery of Mont Parnasse, where the exhumations were carried to such an extent, that the authorities were at their wits' end.

Considering, by the way, that all these cemeteries are surrounded by walls, and have iron gates, which are kept closed, it certainly seems very strange that any ghoul or vampyre of solid flesh and blood should have been able to pursue his vocation so long undiscovered. However, so it was; and it was not till they bethought themselves of laying a snare for this mysterious visitor that he was detected. Having remarked a spot where the wall, though nine feet high, appeared to have been frequently scaled, an old officer contrived a sort of infernal machine, with a wire attached to it, which he so arranged that it should explode if any one attempted to enter the cemetery at that point. This done, and a watch being set, they thought themselves now secure of their purpose.

Accordingly, at midnight, an explosion roused the guardians, who perceived a man already in the cemetery; but before they could seize him, he had leapt the wall with an agility that confounded them; and although they fired their pieces after him, he succeeded in making his escape. But his footsteps were marked with blood that had flowed from his wounds, and several scraps of military attire were picked up on the spot.

Nevertheless, they seem to have been still uncertain where to seek the offender, till one of the grave-diggers of Mont Parnasse, whilst preparing the last resting-place of two criminals about to be executed, chanced to overhear some sappers of the 74th regiment remarking that one of their sergeants had returned on the preceding night cruelly wounded, nobody knew how, and had been conveyed to Val de Grace, which is a military hospital.

A little inquiry now soon cleared up the mystery; and it was ascertained that Sergeant Bertrand was the author of all these profanations, and of many others of the same description previous to his arrival in Paris.

Supported on crutches, wrapped in a grey cloak, pale and feeble, Bertrand was now brought forward for examination; nor was there anything in the countenance or appearance of this young man indicative of the fearful monomania of which he is the victim for the whole tenor of his confession proves that in no other light is his horrible propensity to be considered.

In the first place, he freely acknowledged himself the author of these violations of the dead in both Paris and elsewhere.

"What object did you propose to yourself in committing these acts?" inquired the president.

"I cannot tell," replied Bertrand: "it was a horrible impulse. I was driven to it against my own will: nothing could stop or deter me. I cannot describe or understand myself what my sensations were in tearing and rending these bodies."

President. And what did you do after one of these visits to a cemetery?

Bertrand. I withdrew, trembling convulsively, feeling a great desire for repose. I fell asleep, no matter where, and slept for several hours; but during this sleep I heard everything that passed around me! I have sometimes exhumed from ten to fifteen bodies in a night. I dug them up with my hands, which were often torn and bleeding with the labor, I underwent; but I minded nothing, so that I could get at them. The guardians fired at me one night and wounded me, but that did not prevent my returning the next. This de- sire seized me generally about once a fortnight."

He added that he had had no access of this propensity since he was in the hospital, but that he would not be sure it might not return when his wounds were healed. Still he hoped not. "I think I am cured," said he. "I had never seen any one die; in the hospital I have seen several of my comrades expire by my side. I believe I am cured, for now I fear the dead."

The surgeons who attended him were then examined, and one of them read a sort of memoir he had received from Bertrand, which contained the history of his malady as far as his memory served him.

From these notes, it appears that there had been something singular and abnormal about him from the time he was seven or eight years old. It was not so much in acts, as in his love of solitude and his profound melancholy that the aberration was exhibited and it was not till two years 'ago that his frightful peculiarity fully developed itself Passing a cemetery one day, where the grave-diggers were covering a body that had just been interred, he entered to observe them.

A violent shower of rain interrupted their labors, which they left unfinished. "At this sight," says Bertrand, "horrible desires seized me: my head throbbed, my heart palpitated violently; I excused myself to my companions, and returned hastily into town. No sooner did I find myself alone, than I procured a spade, and returned to the cemetery.

I had just succeeded in exhuming the body, when I saw a peasant watching me at the gate. Whilst he went to inform the authorities of what he had seen, I withdrew, and retiring into a neighboring wood, I laid myself down, and in spite of the torrents of rain that were falling, I remained there in a state of profound insensibility for several hours."

From this period, he appears to have given free course to his inclinations; but as he generally covered the mutilated remains with earth again, it was some time before his proceedings excited observation. He had many narrow escapes of being taken or killed by the pistols of the guardians; but his agility seems to have been almost super-human.

To the living, he was gentle and kind, and was especially beloved in his regiment for his frankness and gaiety the medical men interrogated unanimously gave it as their opinion, that although in all other respects perfectly sane, Bertrand was not responsible for these acts. He was sentenced to a year's imprisonment, during which time measures will doubtless be taken to complete his cure.

In relating this curious case of the Vompyre, as he is called in Paris, where the affair has excited considerable attention, especially in the medical world, I have omitted several painful and disgusting particulars ; but I have said enough to prove that, beyond a doubt, there has been some good foundation for the ancient belief in ghoulism and lycanthropy; and that the books of Dr. Weir and others, in which the existence of this malady is contemptuously denied, have been put forth without due investigation of the subject.

# LYCANTHROPY

## *Legends*

# Legend of the Werewolf

## by **Sabine Baring-Gould**

The plague was raging in Europe, and werewolves and Vampires roamed the night looking for clean victims to fulfill their blood-lust. It was in this time that people were fleeing their homes in the towns to avoid the plague. Most took refuge in the Forests, while others in the Transylvanian Alps. It was in this time and these dark and foreboding mountains that a grizzly event took place...

Bala Bideski and his family had fled their home into the mountains as the plague took a firm grip of their town (they were the last to escape, and some would say later that it was unfortunate that they did). Bala, his wife Chelitha, his two sons Christopher and Thengal, and his daughter Tahlia had set up a comfortable home in the forested hills that surrounded the mountains. One day Bala and his two sons (Chris 14 and Thengal 16) were cutting and gathering wood for the fire as it was almost winter and they'd need a large stockpile to get through the freezing conditions. Chris had wondered off from his father and was getting closer and closer to the steep incline of the mountains rough surface. He was about to return to his father when he heard the whimpering of what sounded like pups. He moved towards the sound, until he came upon a den in a small clearing. There in the mouth of the den were two beautiful pups, one of which looked strangely human. Chris came close to the pups and picked one of them up. After a while of petting the wolf-pup, he put it back on the ground and left the area to find his father and brother.

Not long after the young boy had left, the she-wolf returned to her den to find one of her pups covered in the smell of humans. The father of the pups was a lycanthrope who preferred to stay in wolf form, and he was livid...The lycanthrope had no choice but to kill his pup that had been handled by a human. After he did the deed, the werewolf went looking for the human perpetrator...It wasn't long before he found the trail and followed it to a small hut on the hills in the forest.

It was getting quite late when the family decided to turn in for the night. Chris lay down and his mother doused the lights. In the early hours of the morning came a "howling" that pierced the night. Chris awoke with a start. He looked around the room he shared with his older brother. The moon outside was full so a stream of silver light poured in through the window above his bed, he could see the shadow of a small tree just outside his window against the far wall...But the shadow of the tree changed, in a second, into the shadow of a wolf standing on its hind legs. Except this wolf was huge...Bigger than any man Chris had ever seen.

"Thengal!!!!" Chris whispered, "Wake up!!!"

Thengal stirred under his bed covers then opened his eyes... There at the window, silhouetted by the full moon was a wolf-man...Its eyes burned red and glowed. Thengal sat up in his bed...As he did the creature dived through the window frame and landed on Thengals bed. The werewolf tore at Thengals chest and neck, ripping out vital organs and his windpipe as he did so. By the time, the wolf-creature was through the sixteen-year-old boys body lay in tatters on the bed. The wolf turned to Chris, but as it did the door to the room (a long piece of material) was thrown open and Bala and Chelitha bounded into the room. The werewolf flung its huge body out the window once more. Chelitha ran to her dead son's bed and screamed her sorrow, while Bala grabbed his pitchfork (which he kept at the huts door) and ran out the door... As Bala left the hut, a massive claw knocked him into their winter stockpile of wood, knocking him unconscious. Moments later, he awoke to find the wolf towering over him. The werewolf bent down and let the nail of its index finger to touch Bala's Adams-apple. Then, with one quick flinch of its finger, the wolf-thing sliced along Bala's neck, making him choke on his own blood...Now the wolf-man entered the house once more, this time through the door...

Chelitha's sobs could be heard as the werewolf moved silently through the house to Tahlia's room. The twelve-year-old girl was sound asleep in her bed as the wolf's shadow moved over her body. Tahlia awoke and looked at the creature...She gave a scream as its jaws closed in on her face and slammed shut, in one swift movement, on her face...The wolf-creature stood and spat blood and pieces of flesh and bone onto the dirt floor. Chelitha ran into the room to find her daughters faceless body laying dead on the floor (where she had ended up), and the beast that did it standing there looking at her. Horror and fear shot through her distraught body. She ran back to her son's room and grabbed Chris. They were about to flee the hut, when the wolf-creature stood in the doorway. Chelitha pulled her last remaining child to her breast. Chris closed his eyes and prayed...All remained silent, so he looked up at his mother's face...But her head was gone...Her body fell to the ground with a thud...

Chris looked about his room... Death was everywhere...But there was no wolf-thing...He stumbled through the house and out the door to exit the hut... There he found his dead father...Shocked and frightened, Chris stumbled into the forest, his breath making plumes in the air...

The next summer a group of woodsmen found the rotting corpses in the hut. They new that the family had consisted of two son's so they searched the area, but found no trace...For years the rumor circulated that the young boy, Chris, had gone crazy due to the isolation the family endured and had killed them all...Until over ten years later a group of children playing in the forest found the decayed body of a young boy...The authorities found a necklace around the boys neck, this made identification of the body easier as the necklace was very distinctive...They found that the body was of Chris, the missing child of the massacred family.

This story was reportedly told to a Publican who swore he was told by the thing that did these horrible crimes. Apparently after he was told the story, the Publican was attacked by the man, who "changed" into a wolf-like creature...The thing was frightened off, before it could inflict any injury bar a bump on the head, by a group of hunters who'd heard a commotion behind the pub.

# Sabine Baring-Gould

January 28, 1834 – January 2, 1924

Rev. **Sabine Baring-Gould** (28 January 1834 – 2 January 1924) was an English Anglican priest, hagiographer, antiquarian, novelist and eclectic scholar. His bibliography consists of more than 1240 publications, though this list continues to grow. His family home, Lew Trenchard Manor near Okehampton, Devon, has been preserved as he had it rebuilt and is now a hotel. He is remembered particularly as a writer of hymns, the best known being "Onward, Christian Soldiers", and "Now the Day Is Over." He also translated the carol "Gabriel's Message" from the Basque language to the English.

Baring-Gould wrote many novels including *The Broom-Squire* set in the Devil's Punch Bowl (1896), *Mehalah* and *Guavas, the Tinner* (1897), a collection of ghost stories, a 16-volume *The Lives of the Saints*, and the biography of the eccentric poet-vicar of Morwenstow, Robert Stephen Hawker. His folkloric studies resulted in *The Book of Were-Wolves* (1865); one of the most frequently cited studies of lycanthropy. He habitually wrote while standing, and his desk can be seen in the manor.

One of his most enduringly popular works was *Curious Myths of the Middle Ages*, first published in two parts during 1866 and 1868, and republished in many other editions since then. "Each of the book's twenty-four chapter's deals with a particular medieval superstition and its variants and antecedents," writes critic Steven J. Mariconda. H. P. Lovecraft termed it "that curious body of medieval lore which the late Mr. Baring-Gould so effectively assembled in book form."

He wrote much about the West Country: his works of this topic include:

- *A Book of the West*. 2 vols. I: Devon; II: Cornwall. London : Methuen, 1899

- *Cornish Characters and Strange Events*. London: John Lane, 1909 (reissued in 1925 in 2 vols., First series and Second series)

- *Devonshire Characters and Strange Events*.

Baring-Gould served as President of the Royal Institution of Cornwall for ten years from 1897.

He regarded his principal achievement to be the collection of folk songs that he made with the help of the ordinary people of Devon and Cornwall. His first book of songs, *Songs and Ballads of the West* (1889–91), was published in four parts between 1889 and 1891. The musical editor for this collection was Henry Fleetwood Sheppard, though some of the songs included were noted by Baring-Gould's other collaborator Frederick Bussell.

Baring-Gould and Sheppard produced a second collection named *A Garland of Country Songs* during 1895. A new edition of *Songs of the West* was proposed for publication in 1905. Sheppard had died in 1901 and so the folk song collector Cecil Sharp was invited to undertake the musical editorship for the new edition. Sharp and Baring-Gould also collaborated on *English Folk Songs for Schools* during 1907. This collection of 53 songs was widely used in British schools for the next 60 years.

Although he had to modify the words of some songs, which were too rude for the time, he left his original manuscripts for future students of folk song, thereby preserving many beautiful pieces of music and their lyrics that might otherwise have been lost.

A Fair Copy of the folk songs he collected, together with the notebooks used for gathering information in the field, were given by Baring-Gould to Plymouth Public Library in 1914 and deposited with the Plymouth and West Devon Record Office in 2006. These, together with the folk-song manuscripts from Baring-Gould's personal library discovered at Killerton in 1998, were published as a microfiche edition in 1998. In 2011 the complete collection of folk song manuscripts (including two notebooks not included in the microfiches edition) were digitized and published online by the Devon Tradition Project in association with the English Folk Dance and Song Society as part of the 'Take

Six' project undertaken by the Vaughan Williams Memorial Library. It now forms part of the VWML's 'Full English' website. Thirty boxes of additional manuscript material on other topics (the Killerton manuscripts) are kept in the Devon History Centre in Exeter.

Cecil Sharp dedicated his *English Folk Song— Some Conclusions* to Baring-Gould.

## Lycanthropy and the Ancients

Definition of Lycanthropy--Marcellus Sidetes--Virgil--Herodotus--Ovid--Pliny--Agriopas--Story from Petronius--Arcadian Legends--Explanation offered.

WHAT is Lycanthropy? The change of manor woman into the form of a wolf, either through magical means, so as to enable him or her to gratify the taste for human flesh, or through judgment of the gods in punishment for some great offence.

This is the popular definition. Truly, it consists in a form of madness, such as may be found in most asylums.

Among the ancients, this kind of insanity went by the names of Lycanthropy, Kuanthropy, or Boanthropy, because those afflicted with it believed themselves to be turned into wolves, dogs, or cows. But in the North of Europe, as we shall see, the shape of a bear, and in Africa that of a hyena, were often selected in preference. A mere matter of taste! According to Marcellus Sidetes, of whose poem "περὶ λυκανθρώπου" a fragment exists, men are attacked with this madness chiefly in the beginning of the year, and become most furious in February; retiring for the night to lone cemeteries, and living precisely in the manner of dogs and wolves.

Virgil writes in his eighth Eclogue:--

> Has herbas, atque hæc Ponto mihi lecta venena
> Ipse dedit Mœris; nascuntur plurima Ponto.
> His ego sæpe lupum fieri et se conducere sylvis
> Mœrim, sæpe animas imis excire sepulchris,
> Atque satas alio, vidi traducere messes.

And Herodotus:--"It seems that the Neuri are sorcerers, if one is to believe the Scythians and the Greeks established in Scythia; for each Neurian changes himself, once in the year, into the form of a wolf, and he continues in that form for several days, after which he resumes his former shape."

See also Pomponius Mela. "There is a fixed time for each Neurian, at which they change, if they like, into wolves, and back again into their former condition."

But the most remarkable story among the ancients is that related by Ovid in his "Metamorphoses," of Lycaon, king of Arcadia, who, entertaining Jupiter one day, set before him a hash of human flesh, to prove his omniscience, whereupon the god transferred him into a wolf:

In vain he attempted to speak;
from that very instant
His jaws were be spluttered with
foam, and only he thirsted
For blood, as he raged amongst
flocks and panted for slaughter.
His vesture was changed into hair,
his limbs became crooked;
A wolf,--he retains yet large trace
of his ancient expression,
Hoary he is as afore, his
countenance rabid,
His eyes glitter savagely still, the
picture of fury.

Pliny relates from Evanthes, that on the
festival of Jupiter Lycæus, one of the family of
Antæus was selected by lot, and conducted to
the brink of the Arcadian lake. He then hung
his clothes on a tree and plunged into the
water, whereupon he was transformed into a
wolf. Nine years after, if he had not tasted
human flesh, he was at liberty to swim back
and resume his former shape, which had in
the meantime become aged, as though he had
worn it for nine years.

Agriopas relates, that Demænetus, having
assisted at an Arcadian human sacrifice to
Jupiter Lycæus, ate of the flesh, and was at
once transformed into a wolf, in which shape
he prowled about for ten years, after which he

recovered his human form, and took part in the Olympic Games.

The following story is from Petronius:--

"My master had gone to Capua to sell some old clothes. I seized the opportunity, and persuaded our guest to bear me company about five miles out of town, for he was a soldier, and as bold as death. We set out about cockcrow, and the moon shone bright as day, when, coming among some monuments. my man began to converse with the stars, whilst I jogged along singing and counting them. Presently I looked back after him, and saw him strip and lay his clothes by the side of the road. My heart was in my mouth in an instant, I stood like a corpse; when, in a crack, he was turned into a wolf. Don't think I'm joking: I would not tell you a lie for the finest fortune in the world.

"But to continue: after he was turned into a wolf, he set up a howl and made straight for the woods. At first I did not know whether I was on my head or my heels; but at last going to take up his clothes, I found them turned into stone. The sweat streamed from me, and I never expected to get over it. Melissa began to wonder why I walked so late. 'Had you come a little sooner,' she said, 'you might at least have lent us a hand; for a wolf broke into the farm and has butchered all our cattle; but though be got off, it was no laughing matter for him, for a servant of ours ran him through with a pike. Hearing this I could not close an eye; but as soon as it was daylight, I ran home like a peddler that has been eased of his pack. Coming to the place where the clothes had been turned into stone, I saw nothing but a pool of blood; and when I got home, I found my soldier lying in bed, like an ox in a stall, and a surgeon dressing his neck. I saw at once that he was a fellow who could change his skin (*versipellis*), and never after could I eat bread with him, no, not if you would have killed me. Those who would have taken a different view of the case are welcome to their opinion; if I tell you a lie, may your genii confound me!"

As every one knows, Jupiter changed himself into a bull; Hecuba became a bitch; Actæon a stag; the comrades of Ulysses were transformed into swine; and the daughters of Prœtus fled through the fields believing themselves to be cows, and would not allow any one to come near them, lest they should be caught and yoked.

S. Augustine declared, in his *De Civitate Dei*, that he knew an old woman who was said to turn men into asses by her enchantments.

Apuleius has left us his charming romance of the *Golden Ass*, in which the hero, through injudicious use of a magical salve, is transformed into that long-eared animal.

It is to be observed that the chief seat of Lycanthropy was Arcadia, and it has been very plausibly suggested that the cause might he traced to the following circumstance:--The natives were a pastoral people, and would consequently suffer very severely from the attacks and depredations of wolves. They would naturally institute a sacrifice to obtain deliverance from this pest, and security for their flocks. This sacrifice consisted in the offering of a child, and it was instituted by Lycaon. From the circumstance of the sacrifice being human, and from the peculiarity of the name of its originator, rose the myth.

But, on the other hand, the story is far too widely spread for us to attribute it to an accidental origin, or to trace it to a local source.

Half the world believes, or believed in, were-wolves, and they were supposed to haunt the Norwegian forests by those who had never remotely been connected with Arcadia: and the superstition had probably struck deep its roots into the Scandinavian and Teutonic minds, ages before Lycaon existed; and we have only to glance at Oriental literature, to see it as firmly engrafted in the imagination of the Easterns.

## Werewolves in the Middle Ages

Stories from Olaus Magnus of Livonian Were-wolves--Story from Bishop Majolus--Story of Albertus Pericofcius--Similar occurrence at Prague--Saint Patrick--Strange incident related by John of Nüremberg--Bisclaveret--Courland Were-wolves--Pierre Vidal--Pavian Lycanthropist--Bodin's Stories--Forestus' Account of a Lycanthropist--Neapolitan Were-wolf

OLAUS MAGNUS relates that--"In Prussia, Livonia, and Lithuania, although the inhabitants suffer considerably from the rapacity of wolves throughout the year, in that these animals rend their cattle, which are scattered in great numbers through the woods, whenever they stray in the very least, yet this is not regarded by them as such a serious matter as what they endure from men turned into wolves.

"On the feast of the Nativity of Christ, at night, such a multitude of wolves transformed from men gather together in a certain spot, arranged among themselves, and then spread

153

to rage with wondrous ferocity against human beings, and those animals which are not wild, that the natives of these regions suffer more detriment from these, than they do from true and natural wolves; for when a human habitation has been detected by them isolated in the woods, they besiege it with atrocity, striving to break in the doors, and in the event of their doing so, they devour all the human beings, and every animal which is found within. They burst into the beer-cellars, and there they empty the tunes of beer or mead, and pile up the empty casks one above another in the middle of the cellar, thus showing their difference from natural and genuine wolves. . . Between Lithuania, Livonia, and Courland are the walls of a certain old ruined castle. At this spot congregate thousands, on a fixed occasion, and try their agility in jumping. Those who are unable to bound over the wall, as; is often the case with the fattest, are fallen upon with scourges by the captains and slain." Olaus relates also the story of a certain nobleman who was travelling through a large forest with some peasants in his retinue who dabbled in the black art. They found no house where they could lodge for the night, and were well nigh famished. Then one of the peasants offered, if all the rest would hold their tongues as to what he should do, that he would bring them a lamb from a distant flock.

He thereupon retired into the depths of the forest and changed his form into that of a wolf, fell upon the flock, and brought a lamb to his companions in his mouth. They received it with gratitude. Then he retired once more into the thicket, and transformed himself back again into his human shape.

The wife of a nobleman in Livonia expressed her doubts to one of her slaves whether it were possible for man or woman thus to change shape. The servant at once volunteered to give her evidence of the possibility. He left the room, and in another moment, a wolf was observed running over the country. The dogs followed him, and notwithstanding his resistance, tore out one of his eyes. Next day the slave appeared before his mistress blind of an eye.

At Christmas, a boy lame of a leg goes round the country summoning the devil's followers, who are countless, to a general conclave. Whoever remains behind, or goes reluctantly, is scourged by another with an iron whip till the blood flows, and his traces are left in blood. The human form vanishes, and the whole multitude becomes wolves. Many thousands assemble. Foremost goes the leader armed with an iron whip, and the troop follow, "firmly convinced in their imaginations that they are transformed into wolves." They fall upon herds of cattle and flocks of sheep, but they have no power to slay men. When they come to a river, the leader smites the water with his scourge, and it divides, leaving a dry path through the midst, by which the pack may go. The transformation lasts during twelve days, at the expiration of which period the wolf-skin vanishes, and the human form reappears. This superstition was expressly forbidden by the church. "Credidisti, quod quidam credere solent, ut illæ quæ a vulgo Parcæ vocantur, ipsæ, vel sint vel possint hoc facere quod creduntur, id est, dum aliquis homo nascitur, et tunc valeant illum designare ad hoc quod velint, ut quandocunque homo ille voluerit, in lupum transformari possit, quod vulgaris stultitia, *werwolf* vocat, aut in aliam aliquam figuram?"--Ap. Burchard. (d. 1024). In like manner did S. Boniface preach against those who believed superstitiously in it strigas et fictos lupos."

In a dissertation by Müller, we learn, on the authority of Cluverius and Dannhaverus (*Acad. Homilet.* p. ii.), that a certain Albertus Pericofcius in Muscovy was wont to tyrannize over and harass his subjects in the most unscrupulous manner. One night when he was, absent from home, his whole herd of cattle, acquired by extortion, and perished. On his return he was informed of his loss, and the wicked man broke out into the most horrible

156

blasphemies, exclaiming, "Let him who has slain, eat; if God chooses, let him devour me as well."

As he spoke, drops of blood fell to earth, and the nobleman, transformed into a wild dog, rushed upon his dead cattle, tore and mangled the carcasses and began to devour them; possibly, he may be devouring them still (*ac forsan hodie que pascitur*). His wife, then near her confinement, died of fear. Of these circumstances, there was not only ear but also eyewitnesses. (*Non ab auritis tantum, sed et ocidatis accepi, quodnarro*). Similarly it is related of a nobleman in the neighbourhood of Prague, that he robbed his subjects of their goods and reduced them to penury through his exactions. He took the last cow from a poor widow with five children, but as a judgment, all his own cattle died. He then broke into fearful oaths, and God transformed him into a dog: his human head, however, remained.

S. Patrick is said to have changed Vereticus, king of Wales, into a wolf, and S. Natalis, the abbot, to have pronounced anathema upon an illustrious family in Ireland; in consequence of which, every male and female take the form of wolves for seven years and live in the forests and career over the bogs, howling mournfully, and appeasing their hunger upon the sheep of the peasants. A duke of Prussia, according to Majolus, had a countryman brought for sentence before him, because he had devoured his neighbour's cattle. The fellow was an ill-favoured, deformed man, with great wounds in his face, which he had received from dogs' bites whilst he had been in his wolf's form. It was believed that he changed shape twice in the year, at Christmas and at Midsummer. He was said to exhibit much uneasiness and discomfort when the wolf-hair began to break out and his bodily shape to change.

He was kept long in prison and closely watched, lest he should become a were-wolf during his confinement and attempt to escape, but nothing remarkable took place. If this is the same individual as that mentioned by Olaus Magnus, as there seems to be a probability, the poor fellow was burned alive.

John of Nüremberg relates the following curious story: a priest was once travelling in a strange country, and lost his way in a forest. Seeing a fire, he made towards it, and beheld a wolf seated over it. The wolf addressed him in human-voice, and bade him not fear, as "he was of the Ossyrian race, of which a man and a woman were doomed to spend a certain number of years in wolf's form. Only after seven years might they return home and resume their former shapes, if they were still alive." He begged the priest to visit and console his sick wife, and to give her the last sacraments. This the priest consented to do, after some hesitation, and only when convinced of the beasts being human beings, by observing that the wolf used his front paws as hands, and when he saw the she-wolf peel off her wolf-skin from her head to her navel, exhibiting the features of an aged woman.

Marie de France says in the Lais du Bisclaveret:

> Bisclaveret ad nun en Bretan
> Garwall Papelent li Norman.
>
> \*   \*   \*   \*
>
> Jadis le poet-hum oir Et souvent suleit avenir, Humes pluseirs Garwall deviendrent E es boscages meisun tindrent

There is an interesting paper by Rhanæus, on the Courland were-wolves, in the Breslauer Sammlung. The author says,--"There are too many examples derived not merely from hearsay, but received on indisputable evidence, for us to dispute the fact, that Satan--if we do not deny that such a being exists, and that he has his work in the children of darkness--holds the Lycanthropists in his net in three ways:--

"1. They execute as wolves certain acts, such as seizing a sheep, or destroying cattle, &c., not changed into wolves, which no scientific man in Courland believes, but in their human frames, and with their

1. An epitome of this curious were-wolf tale will be found in Ellis's *Early English Metrical Romances*.

2. Supplement III. *Curieuser* und nutzbarer Anmerkungen von Natur und Kunstgeschichten, gesammelt von Kanold. 1728.] human limbs, yet in such a state of phantasy and hallucination, that they believe themselves transformed into wolves, and are regarded as such by others suffering under similar hallucination, and in this manner run these people in packs as wolves, though not true wolves.

"2. They imagine, in deep sleep or dream, that they injure the cattle, and this without leaving their conch; but it is their master who does, in their stead, what their fancy points out, or suggests to him.

"3. The evil one drives natural wolves to do some act, and then pictures it so well to the sleeper, immovable in his place, both in dreams and at awaking, that he believes the act to have been committed by himself."

Rhanæus, under these heads, relates three stories, which he believes be has on good authority. The first is of a gentleman starting on a journey, who came upon a wolf engaged in the act of seizing a sheep in his own flock; he fired at it, and wounded it, so that it fled howling to the thicket. When the gentleman returned from his expedition, he found the whole neighbourhood impressed with the belief that he had, on a given day and hour, shot at one of his tenants, a publican, Mickel. On inquiry, the man's Wife, called Lebba, related the following circumstances, which were fully corroborated by numerous witnesses:--When her husband had sown his rye, he had consulted with his wife how he was to get some meat, so as to have a good feast. The woman urged him on no account to steal from his landlord's flock, because it was guarded by fierce dogs. He, however, rejected her advice, and Mickel fell upon his landlord's sheep, but he had suffered and had come limping home, and in his rage at the ill success of his attempt, had fallen upon his own horse and had bitten its throat completely through. This took place in the year 1684.

In 1684, a man was about to fire upon a pack of wolves, when he heard from among the troop a voice exclaiming--"Gossip! Gossip! don't fire. No good will come of it."

The third story is as follows:--A lycanthropist was brought before a judge and accused of witchcraft, but as nothing could be proved against him, the judge ordered one of his peasants to visit the man in his prison, and to worm the truth out of him, and to persuade the prisoner to assist him in revenging himself upon another peasant who had injured him; and this was to be effected by destroying one of the man's cows; but the peasant was to urge the prisoner to do it secretly, and, if possible, in the disguise of a wolf. The fellow undertook the task, but he had great difficulty in persuading the prisoner to fall in with his wishes: eventually, however, he succeeded. Next morning the cow was found in its stall frightfully mangled, but the prisoner had not left his cell: for the watch, who had been placed to observe him, declared that he had spent the night in profound sleep, and that he had only at one time made a slight motion with his head and hands and feet.

Wierius and Forestus quote Gulielmus Brabantinus as an authority for the fact, that a man of high position had been so possessed by the evil one, that often during the year he fell into a condition in which he believed himself to be turned into a wolf, and at that time he roved in the woods and tried to seize and devour little children, but that at last, by God's mercy, he recovered his senses.

Certainly the famous Pierre Vidal, the Don Quixote of Provençal troubadours, must have had a touch of this madness, when, after having fallen in love with a lady of Carcassone, named Loba, or the Wolfess, the excess of his passion drove him over the country, howling like a wolf, and demeaning himself more like an irrational beast than a rational man.

He commemorates his lupine madness in the poem *A Tal Donna*:

> Crowned with immortal joys I mount
> The proudest emperors above,
> For I am honored with the love
> Of the fair daughter of a count.
> A lace from Na Raymbauda's hand
> I value more than all the land
> Of Richard, with his Poïctou,
> His rich Touraine, and famed Anjou.
>
> When *loup-garou* the rabble call me,
> When vagrant shepherds hoot,
> Pursue, and buffet me to boot,
> It doth not for a moment gall me;
> I seek not palaces or halls,
> Or refuge when the winter falls;
> Exposed to winds and frosts at night,

My soul is ravished with delight.
Me claims my she-wolf (*Loba*) so divine:
And justly she that claim prefers,
For, by my troth, my life is hers
More than another's, more than mine.

Job Fincelius relates the sad story of a farmer of Pavia, who, as a wolf, fell upon many men in the open country and tore them to pieces. After much trouble, the maniac was caught, and he then assured his captors that the only difference, which existed between himself and a natural wolf, was that in a true wolf the hair grew outward, whilst in him it struck inward. In order to put this assertion to the proof, the magistrates, himself or herself most certainly cruel and bloodthirsty wolves, cut off his arms and legs; the poor wretch died of the mutilation. This took place in 1541. The idea of the skin being reversed is a very ancient one: *versipellis* occurs as a name of reproach in Petronius, Lucilius, and Plautus, and resembles the Norse *hamrammr*.

Fincelius relates also that, in 1542, there was such a multitude of were-wolves about Constantinople that the Emperor, accompanied by his guard, left the city to give them a severe correction, and slew one hundred and fifty of them.

Spranger speaks of three young ladies who attacked a laborer, under the form of cats, and were wounded by him. They were found bleeding in their beds next morning.

Majolus relates that a man afflicted with lycanthropy was brought to Pomponatius. The poor fellow had been found buried in hay, and when people approached, he called to them to flee, as he was a werewolf, and would rend them. The country-folk wanted to flay him, to discover whether the hair grew inwards, but Pomponatius rescued the man and cured him.

Bodin tells some were-wolf stories on good authority; it is a pity that the good authorities of Bodin were such liars, but that, by the way. He says that the Royal Procurator-General Bourdin had assured him that he had shot a wolf, and that the arrow had stuck in the beast's thigh. A few hours after, the arrow was found in the thigh of a man in bed. In Vernon, about the year 1566, the witches and warlocks gathered in great multitudes, under the shape of cats. Four or five men were attacked in a lone place by a number of these beasts. The men stood their ground with the utmost heroism, succeeded in slaying one puss, and in wounding many others. Next day a number of wounded women were found in the town, and they gave the judge an accurate account of all the circumstances connected with their wounding.

Bodin quotes Pierre Marner, the author of a treatise on sorcerers, as having witnessed in Savoy the transformation of men into wolves. Nynauld relates that in a village of Switzerland, near Lucerne, a wolf attacked a peasant, whilst he was hewing timber; he defended himself, and smote off a foreleg of the beast. The moment that the blood began to flow the wolf's form changed, and he recognized a woman without her arm. She was burned alive.

Evidence that beasts are transformed witches is to be found in their having no tails. When the devil takes human form, however, he keeps his clubfoot of the Satyr, as a token by which he may be recognized. So animals deficient in caudal appendages are to be avoided, as they are witches in disguise. The thing Wald should consider the case of the Manx cats in its next session.

Forestus, in his chapter on maladies of the brain, relates a circumstance, which came under his own observation, in the middle of the sixteenth century, at Alcmaar in the Netherlands. A peasant there was attacked every spring with a fit of insanity; under the influence of this he rushed about the churchyard, ran into the church, jumped over the benches, danced, was filled with fury, climbed up, descended, and never remained quiet. He carried a long staff in his hand, with which he drove away the dogs, which flew at him and wounded him, so that his thighs were covered with scars. His face was pale, his eyes deep sunk in their sockets. Forestus pronounces the man to be a lycanthropist, but he does not say that the poor fellow believed himself to be transformed into a wolf. In reference to this case, however, he mentions that of a Spanish nobleman who believed himself to be changed into a bear, and who wandered filled with fury among the woods.

Donatus of Altomare affirms that he saw a man in the streets of Naples, surrounded by a ring of people, who in his were-wolf frenzy had dug up a corpse and was carrying off the leg upon his shoulders. This was in the middle of the sixteenth century.

# 4

## The Ultimate Role Playing Game

## <u>Werewolf</u>

◇◇◇

(Not a computer game – a one-on-one,
up-close-and-personal table game between friends.)

Time for a game of Werewolf! Never heard of it? No bother – let me fill you in.

*Werewolf* is an old role-playing party game, one that probably isn't played as often now, with the invention of video games and such, but is still fun none-the-less. And the cool part – it's now being played on twitter.

But let's get to the game . . .

Werewolf is a pretty simple game for a large group of people (seven or more), and great for large family gatherings. It requires nothing more than players, and a few pieces of paper. Once the players show up, get the paper, and get ready for some accusations, lying, and bluffing, second-guessing, assassination, and mob hysteria . . . *Party!!*

**The Rules**

Getting Set Up

Get a group of players. An odd number is best, although not absolutely necessary. There should be at least seven players; nine or eleven is better (or more if you round them up).

Make up a set of cards (pieces of scrap paper will do fine), one for each player, with a role written on each one: (Examples below.)

- One "Narrator"

- Two "Werewolf"
- One "Seer"
- All the rest get "Villager" cards

Shuffle the cards and hand them out, face down. Each player should look at his card, but must keep it secret. Only the narrator reveals his card, and shows himself to be the narrator.

(Alternatively, the group can choose a narrator in advance; the narrator then takes the "narrator" card, shuffles the rest, and hands them out face-down.)

Two players are now "secretly" werewolves, and they're trying to slaughter everyone in the village. Everyone else is an innocent human villager; but one of the villagers secretly has Second Sight, and can detect the stain of lycanthropy.

## The Game: Night and Day

The game proceeds in alternating night and day phases. *We begin with Night.*

At Night, the narrator tells all the players "Close your eyes." Everyone should.

The narrator says, "Werewolves, open your eyes." The two werewolves do so, and look around to recognize each other. The narrator should also note who the werewolves are.

The narrator says, "Werewolves, pick someone to kill." The two werewolves silently agree on one villager to tear limb from limb. (It is critical that they remain silent. The other players are sitting there with their eyes closed, and the werewolves don't want to give themselves away. Sign language is appropriate, or just pointing, nodding, raising eyebrows, and so on.)

When the werewolves have agreed on a victim, and the narrator understands whom they picked, the narrator says, "Werewolves, close your eyes."

The narrator says "Seer, open your eyes. Seer, pick someone to ask about." The seer opens his eyes and silently points at another player. (Again, it is critical that this be entirely silent — because the seer doesn't want to reveal his identity to the werewolves.)

The narrator silently signs thumbs-up if the seer pointed at a werewolf, and thumbs-down if the seer pointed at an innocent villager. The narrator then says, "Seer, close your eyes."

The narrator says, "Everybody open your eyes; it's daytime. And you have been torn apart by werewolves." (He indicates the person that the werewolves chose.) That person is immediately dead and out of the game. He reveals his card, showing what he was, and leaves it face-up.

Now it is Day. Daytime is very simple; all the living players gather in the village – and lynch somebody. *The mob wants bloody justice.*

As soon as a majority of players votes for a particular player to die, the narrator says, "Ok, you're dead." That player then reveals his card, and the rest of the players find out whether they've lynched a human, a werewolf, or (oops!) the seer.

There are no restrictions on speech. Any living player can say anything he wants — truth, misdirection, nonsense, or barefaced lie.

Inversely, dead players may not speak at all. As soon as the sun comes up and the narrator indicates that someone is dead, he may not speak for the rest of the game. No dying monologues allowed. Similarly, as soon as a majority vote indicates that a player has been lynched, *he is dead.* If he wants to protest his innocence or reveal some information (like the seer's visions), he has to do it before the vote goes through.

No player may reveal his card, to anyone, except when he is killed. All you can do is talk.

Once a player is lynched, night falls and the cycle repeats. Everyone closes their eyes, the werewolves (or werewolf) secretly select someone to kill, the seer (if alive) secretly learns another player's status; then the sun rises, one player is found dead, and the remaining players begin to discuss another lynching. Repeat until one side wins.

## Winning

The humans win if they kill both werewolves.

The werewolves win if they kill enough villagers so that the numbers are even. (Two werewolves and two humans, or one werewolf and one human.) At that point, they can rise up and slaughter the villagers openly. *Yeah!*

## In Case of Confusion

The villagers are trying to figure out who's a werewolf; the werewolves are pretending to be villagers, and trying to throw suspicion on the real villagers.

The seer is trying to throw suspicion on any werewolves he discovers, but without revealing himself to be the seer (because if he does, the werewolves will almost certainly kill him that night, since he's the greatest threat to werewolf national security.) Of course, the seer can reveal himself at any time, if he thinks it's worthwhile to tell the other players what he's learned. Also of course, a werewolf can claim to be the seer, and "reveal" anything he wants. *Lying dog!*

The only information the villagers have, is what other players say — and of course who dies. Accusing someone of being a werewolf is suspicious. Not accusing anyone is also suspicious. Agreeing with another player way suspicious, and therefore so is pretending not to agree with another player. (Who's on first?!) Never voting to kill a particular player is very suspicious for both of them — unless it's the seer, who knows that player is innocent.

### Extras

When everyone closes their eyes at night, it is best for people to start humming, tapping the table, rocking back and forth, or some such noise. This will cover up any accidental sounds that are made by the werewolves, the seer, or the narrator.

The narrator should stick to the script to avoid mistakes or clues. If he says, "Open your eyes, werewolves," instead of "Werewolves, open your eyes," a player may misconstrue the command before the last word.

The narrator should be careful to talk towards the center of the group. If (for example) he turns to face the seer when he says, "Seer, select someone," the werewolves may detect the change in acoustics. *Got it?*

It is really important that dead players not speak, and the narrator not speak outside his official capacity — even to correct a blatant misstatement about a matter of record.

There are several reasons to have an odd number of players (including the narrator): there will be an odd number of living players during each day, which prevents tie votes on lynching's; and the game will always end with a lynching. If there is an even number of players, you can get ties, and the game will end with a nighttime murder —, which is anticlimactic, because everyone knows when the sun goes down that, the game will end at dawn. (Why? Because the werewolves are certain to kill a human and win.)

But more importantly, the humans' chances are significantly weaker when there is an even number of players (including the narrator.) This is probably because an even game always ends with a nighttime murder, and an extra murder is always to the advantage of the wolves, whereas an extra daytime lynching could help either side.

This game can produce a lot of shouting (during the day) and a lot of humming (at night.) Don't play where the neighbors will complain. (Try explaining to the cops at the door: "Don't mind us, we're just deciding who to kill!") *Taser anyone?!*

You can make your cards special if you like; make them more than a scrap of paper. Make them artsy or whatever.

This game has several versions – but here you have the basics. Any way you play it – you're in for a *howling* good time!

# Games for Everyone

## Alphabet Animal Game

Get all the kids/adults in a circle and select one to go first. This player has to say the name of an animal that starts with the letter "A," such as ant or ant or antelope. If the player says, "ant," the next player in the circle has to say a name the starts with the last letter of that word, which would be "T." So, the next player could say, "Turtle" or "Tarantula." Each player has to say the name of an animal that starts with the last letter of the animal said by the player before him. This can be played as an activity for fun, or you can eliminate players if they can't think of a word. The last player standing wins the game.

## Wolfish Hide and Seek

Choose a player to be "it/the werewolf," and have all the other players hide their eyes. The players hiding their eyes are "the seekers/or villagers" who must count to 100, while the player chosen to be "the werewolf" finds a hiding spot. After "the seekers/villagers" count to 100, they all start looking for the "it/werewolf" player. If a "seeker/villager" finds "it/the werewolf," he has to hide with him and is *eaten!* Each player who finds "it/the werewolf" must hide with them and be eaten. The last player to find "it/the werewolf" is of course *just bitten*, and therefore, becomes the "it/werewolf" player for the next game.

**Sponge Relay Race (wet fun!)**

Split players into teams of two, and give each team a sponge. Mark a starting line and finish line about 25 feet away from one another, and place a bucket full of water for each team at the starting line, while placing an empty bucket for each team at the finish line. Saying "Race" starts the game, and the first player in each team line must dip the sponge in water, and race to their team bucket. They must squeeze as much water as they can in their team's empty bucket from the sponge. After they squeeze out the sponge, they race the sponge back to the next player in line. The first team to fill up their team's bucket with water – wins the game.

Floating Balls **(might need napkins to control drooling)**

Hand each player a straw and a Ping-Pong ball (or miniature polystyrene foam ball). Have the children/adults tilt back their heads (looking at the ceiling) and blow through the straw creating a stream of air. As they blow, each player places their ball on the direct stream of air, which makes the ball float freely in the air. After everyone practices, have them compete to see who can make their ball float the longest.

**Keep Away**

The rules are simply elementary (my dear Watson), but the activity is not! Be sure to set a time limit.

Choose up players on two sides in equal teams, their heights should be evenly matched. Each /adult chooses his counterpart on the other team – one-one-one. (Help them rearrange if there is a great disparity in height, age, power, etc. between the two opponents.) Afterwards, have them spread out evenly over the field (room or gym).

As a ball is passed from one teammate to another. The opponents try to snatch the ball from their counterpart. There will be lots of bobbing, jumping, weaving, twisting, and turning. No physical contact with their counterpart is allowed.

Each successful throw or pass between teammates counts as one point. The players keep score aloud as they play. The winners are the group that has the highest total at the end of the time limit.

**Tug-o'-War**

Make sure you're wearing play clothes (you're not going to the Opera) and be prepared for dirt and grime.

Have the kids/adults divide into two equal teams. Each team selects a captain. Now, a line is drawn in the center of the playing area. Have the captains of each team face each other with the line between them (each staying about 3 feet behind the line a) with their team lining up in single file behind them.

Have the players on each team spread out and grab hold of a long rope. When the captains signal to start, the teams pull with all their might, against the other team who is pulling with all of theirs.

Who wins? The team who is the first to drag the other leader over the line! Great fun with lots of yelling and grunting! To make things really interesting – try it on a Slip-n-Slide or *just wet grass, will do!*

## Horse *(Or use any name you like – even Werewolf!)*

You'll need a ball and basketball hoop.

Have the kids/adults line up. The first one in line makes any kind of basketball shot he wants (but he must call the shot first) and the next player must imitate the throw. It can be a silly shot from between the legs, or a regular shot, or a bank shot, etc., any kind of shot that makes it into the hoop is legal (except being lifted up to make it – *not kosher!*).

Each player that successfully makes the shot, escapes getting a letter, and moves to the end of the line, with the next player repeating the same shot. But – whoever misses gets the letter "H", and moves to the end of the line. After a miss, the next player gets to choose how they will make the shot.

The first player who collects H-O-R-S-E loses.

### Frisbee Golf *(outdoor game)*

This game is very similar to miniature golf!

You'll need paper and pencil to keep score, and a Frisbee, *or two!*

Have the first player select the first "hole," it can be an object about 50 feet away at which to aim the Frisbee (tree, bush, or pole . . . ).

Now, everyone gets a turn and counts the number of throws it takes to reach the object, and write down the scores.

Have the next in line pick the next "hole/object" (use all the holes equally) and continue playing.

The winner is the player with the lowest number of tosses.

# Recipes for Wolfish Appetites

## 5

(The family that cooks together – *eats* together!)

∞

# Down Mexico Way

## *Biscuit Casserole*

**Prep time:** 15 min **Cook time:** 25 min **Servings:** 6

## Ingredients

- 1 ½ lb ground beef
- 1 can (10 oz.) diced tomatoes with green chilies
- 2 cups corn
- 2 cans (15–16 oz.) ranch style beans
- 1½ cups shredded cheddar
- 2 cups biscuit baking mix
- ½ cup water

## Preparation

1. Preheat oven to 375° F.

2. Cook ground beef and tomatoes in large skillet until beef is browned.

3. Mix in corn, beans, and ½ cup of the cheese.

4. Pour mixture into casserole dish.

5. Combine baking mix and water in a medium bowl, and pour over the meat/bean mixture.

6. Top with remaining cheese and bake for 25 minutes.

# Old Fashioned Hot Chocolate

Ages: 10 plus

You'll Need:

4 white marshmallows
4 pink marshmallows
2 tablespoons of cocoa
3 tablespoons of sugar
a dash of salt
1/2 cup of hot water
2 1/2 cups of milk

Place cocoa, sugar, and salt in a saucepan, add hot water and stir well. You'll heat on the burner until boiling, stir constantly. Now, turn down the heat, and add milk. Keep stirring while heating the milk – you don't want to boil the milk. Once the mixture is heated, pour it into 4 mugs. Top it off with one pink and one white marshmallow and share with friends.

# Wacky Mac

**Prep time:** 25 min **Cook time:** 30 min
**Servings:** 6

## Ingredients

- 1 box (16 oz.) elbow macaroni (white or wheat)

- 2-3 Tbsp. olive oil and/or butter

- 1 clove garlic, minced

- 1 medium sweet onion (Vidalia or Walla Walla), diced

- 3 Tbsp. flour

- 2 cups milk

- 1 can (14 oz.) artichoke hearts, drained and coarsely chopped

- 1 cup shredded mozzarella

- 1 small log (4-5 oz.) goat cheese

- salt and pepper

- ½ cup bread crumbs (Panko style recommended)

- grated Parmesan

## Preparation

1. Cook macaroni al dente, drain and set aside.

2. Meanwhile, preheat oven to 350° F and grease a 9 x 13 casserole dish.

3. In a large saucepan, heat olive oil and/or butter over medium heat.

4. Add the onions to the butter and sauté until soft. Add garlic and sauté one or two minutes more.

5. Sprinkle in flour and cook about a minute while stirring.

6. Whisk in milk and bring slowly to a simmer. Stir in artichoke hearts.

7. Turn off heat and add mozzarella and goat cheese. Stir until cheese is melted.

8. Add pasta and combine thoroughly. Add salt and pepper to taste.

9. Transfer to casserole dish. Top with breadcrumbs and Parmesan.

   Bake, uncovered, 30–35 minutes, until breadcrumbs are browned.

# Coconut Ice Is Nice

Age: 8 plus (with supervision)

You'll Need:

4 tablespoons cream cheese
3 cups of icing sugar
1/2 cup of coconut
2 teaspoons milk
2 drops of vanilla essence
2 drops of red food coloring


You'll grease a square tin. Now beat the cream cheese until it's smooth, add icing sugar, and milk, and continue to beat slowly. Whip in the vanilla and coconut – until the mixture becomes very stiff.  Now place half the mixture in the greased tin, and mix in the red food coloring with the remaining mixture, and spread the pink half of the mixture over the top of the white half.

You'll chill the mixture in the fridge until cold and firm, then cut into small squares for serving.

# Cheesy Bacon Apple Frittata

**Prep time:** 20 min **Cook time:** 20 min
**Servings:** 4

## Ingredients

- 2 tsp. butter
- 1 apple, peeled and sliced thinly
- 4 eggs
- 2 egg whites
- 2 Tbsp. water
- ½ cup grated cheddar cheese
- Salt
- Pepper

- 4 strips precooked bacon

## Preparation

1. Preheat broiler.

2. Melt butter over medium-high heat in a 10-inch ovenproof skillet.

3. Add apple slices and sauté approximately 12 minutes or until soft.

4. Meanwhile, in a large bowl, whisk eggs, egg whites and water until frothy. Stir in cheese, salt, and pepper.

5. Place bacon strips on top of apples.

6. Pour egg mixture into skillet. Cook 2 minutes, or until bottom and sides are set. Resist the urge to stir!

7. Carefully transfer skillet to broiler and cook, 6 inches from heat, for 2–3 minutes or until top is set.

8. Cut into wedges and serve.

# Nana's Oaty Cookies

Age: 10 plus (without supervision)

You'll Need:

1 cup sugar
¾ cup butter
1 egg
1 cup mashed bananas
1¾ cup oats (quick oats are OK)
1½ cups flour
½ teaspoon salt
¾ teaspoon cinnamon
½ teaspoon baking soda

You'll preheat the oven to 180° C and grease a cooking tray.

Mix the butter, sugar and egg. It will become light and fluffy. After it's creamed together, stir in the mashed bananas and the oats. Now, combine the remaining dry ingredients and add to the creamed mixture. Blend everything well.

Using a teaspoon, measure out the cookie dough onto the greased tray.

One teaspoon makes one cookie, if you want bigger cookies, use a tablespoon.

Now bake for 15-20 minutes, allow for cooling, and serve.

# Gimme That Corn Fritter!

*If you don't smack your lips over this – you ain't alive!*

## Ingredients:

3 egg yolks
1 2/3 cups cooked or canned whole grain corn (preferably non-GMO corn!)
½ teaspoon salt
1/8 teaspoon pepper
¼ cup sifted all-purpose flour
3 egg whites
6 Tablespoons vegetable oil

Makes 6 servings

## Directions:

1. Beat egg yolks until light, then add corn, and next 3 ingredients.

2. Fold in stiffly beaten egg whites. Drop by the spoonful into hot oil in a skillet.

3. Cook on both sides until brown and done.

# Grandma's Scrambled Eggs

You'll Need:

3 eggs
1/4 cup of milk (regular, half & half or cream diluted with water)
1/4 of a teaspoon of salt
a sprinkle of pepper (regular or ground)
parsley (or chopped green onion)
1 tablespoon of butter or oil (or equal)

Break the eggs into a bowl; add milk, salt, and pepper. You want to beat the egg mixture well, (beating make the mixture fluffy). Now get a medium size skillet and spread the oil or butter over the inside surface, poor in the mixture in the skillet and place on the stove's burner (over medium heat), and stir constantly (or it will burn). As the mixture starts to thicken, reduce the heat and keep stirring. Be careful not to over cook – the eggs should be light and fluffy (or a little runny depending upon how you like your scrambled eggs). Use the parsley or chopped green onion as a garnish on top. You can even add a sprinkle of shredded cheese. Yum!

Serve with toast and enjoy!

# Fruity Tooty Kabobs

Ages: 4 plus (with supervision)

Time to get creative!

You'll Need:

Bamboo skewers
1 cup of strawberries
1 cup of thickly sliced banana
A handful of grapes
1 cup of cubed apple pieces
1 cup of pineapple cubes
1 cup of melon cubes (Honeydew or Cantaloupe)

Take 6 in. (15 cm/0.39 inches) long skewers,

and thread the fruit onto them – be creative, mix them up for fun!

Serve these marvelous kabobs with your favorite flavor of yoghurt on the side.

# Football Chili

## Ingredients:

3¼ pound ground chuck
1 medium green bell pepper, chopped
3 (14½ ounce) cans diced tomatoes with garlic and onion, undrained
3 (10¾ ounce) cans tomato soup
1 (16 ounce) can light red kidney beans, rinsed and drained
1 (6 ounce) can tomato paste
5 tablespoons chili powder
1 teaspoon freshly ground black pepper
½ teaspoon paprika

Toppings:
Sour cream
Shredded Cheddar cheese

Chopped green onions
Sliced black olives
Corn chips

## Directions:

1. Cook ground chuck in a large nonstick skillet over medium-high heat 12 to 14 minutes or until meat crumbles and is no longer pink; drain.

2. Place meat in a 5- to 6-quart slow cooker; stir in ½-cup water, green bell peppers, and next 7 ingredients. Cover and cook on high 4 hours. Serve with desired toppings.

## Lollipop Cake

Ages: 5 plus (with supervision)

You'll Need:

100g of melted butter (just under ½ cup)
1 packet of malt biscuits (lots of brands)
1/2 a can of condensed milk
1 pack of fruit puffs or marshmallows (cut up into bits)
Lollipops (your choice of flavors)
Dried coconut (a little or a lot, but not too much)


Crush the biscuits finely.
Chop up the lollipops.
You'll combine with half a can of condensed milk – and mix this well. Now roll the mixture

into a log, and roll the log in the coconut.
OK – you're almost there! Now, place the log
in the fridge, and when it's hard, you'll cut it
into slices for serving.
And enjoy!

# Speedy Lip-Smackin' Lasagna

Total Time: 30 min Prep: 10 min Cook: 20 min

Yield: 4 servings

Easy Family Cooking Recipe

Ingredients

Kosher salt
7 lasagna noodles (about 4 ounces)
1 tablespoon extra-virgin olive oil, plus more

for drizzling
1 pound ground meatloaf mix, such as beef, pork and veal
2 cups tomato sauce
1/8 teaspoon red pepper flakes
3 cups baby spinach
1/3 cup ricotta cheese
1 cup shredded mozzarella cheese
6 tablespoons grated parmesan cheese
1/4 cup thinly sliced fresh basil

Directions

Preheat the broiler. Fill a wide pot with 3 inches of salted water and bring to a boil. Add the noodles and cook until al dente, about 11 minutes, then drain, transfer to a cutting board and halve crosswise.

Meanwhile, heat the olive oil in a large skillet over medium-high heat. Add the ground meat and cook, stirring, until browned. Add the tomato sauce and red pepper flakes and simmer 5 minutes. Add the spinach and stir until it wilts, then add the ricotta and bring to a low simmer. Season with salt and remove from the heat. Toss the mozzarella and 4 tablespoons parmesan in a bowl.

Cover the bottom of an 8-inch-square baking dish with a layer of slightly overlapping lasagna noodles. Top with half of the meat sauce and half of the cheese mixture. Repeat with another layer of noodles and the remaining meat sauce and cheese mixture. Cover with the remaining noodles and sprinkle with the remaining 2 tablespoons parmesan. Drizzle lightly with olive oil and broil until golden and bubbling, 3 to 5 minutes. Top with the basil.

Per serving: Calories 671; Fat 33 g (Saturated 14 g); Cholesterol 123 mg; Sodium 747 mg; Carbohydrate 49 g; Fiber 5 g; Protein 44 g

## Saucy Cheesy Toasties Pleasey

**Ages:** 10 plus

You'll Need:

2 tablespoons of butter (or equal)
1 cup of grated cheese (your favorite)
1/4 cup of chutney (your favorite brand)
1 tablespoon grated onion/green onions OK)
1 tablespoon of tomato sauce (not tomato paste)
1 tablespoon Worcestershire sauce
6 thick slices of bread (Texas Toast is great, but your favorite bread works too!)
Turn the grill on high. Melt butter in a small pan and stir in the cheese and chutney.
Add onion, tomato sauce, & Worcestershire sauce. Now stir and mix well. Place the bread

under the grill, and lightly toast one side. You'll spread the cheese mixture on the untoasted side. Now place the toast with cheesy spread under the grill until it's bubbly golden brown. Serve immediately – *'cause you can't wait!*

# Garlic Bread

**Ages:** 10 plus

You'll Need:
Butter (or equal)
Garlic salt/or garlic powder & salt mixture OK
French bread (half a loaf)
(Just double the recipe to share with more folks)
Turn the oven on to 150°c or 300°f.
Cut the French bread into 3 serving sizes. Split each piece into 2 by slicing through the middle. Butter the bread, then lightly sprinkle with garlic salt. Place in oven until golden brown.

# SMOOTHIE HEAVEN

# Citrus Blast

1 lemon squeezed
1 orange squeezed
4 tablespoons of lemon juice (squeezed is better, but it can be concentrate)
1/4 grapefruit (no pits)
2 tablespoons salt
1/2 teaspoon sugar (or equal)
6 ice cubes
1/2 cup water (from the tap or filtered)

# Banana Fanna Smoothie

You'll Need:

1.5 frozen bananas (buy frozen or freeze after peeling in plastic bag)
8 ounces milk (fresh, condensed, or ½ cream ½ water)

Combine ingredients in blender. Blend everything until smooth. You might add more bananas at this point if you want your smoothie thicker.

If you like strawberries – throw them in too!

## Nutter Butter Banana Smoothie

You'll Need:

1.5 frozen banana (freeze your own or buy frozen)
8 ounces of milk (almond milk is good too, sweetened is best for this)
2 tbs. peanut butter (chunky or smooth)


Mix all ingredients in the blende, and blend until the mixture is smooth.

## Chocolate Banana Smoothie

You'll need:

1.5 frozen bananas (you can freeze your own)
8 ounces chocolate milk (make your own with
chocolate syrup and regular milk)
Blend it all together until smooth!
You can even add peanut butter or nuts if you
like.

Top it off with whip cream and Enjoy!

## Legal Stuff

Any likeness to those living or dead is merely coincidental, except where intended.

## About the Author

Lyn Murray writes for you, the reader.

She is fascinated by anything that has to do with the supernatural, the paranormal. This led her to become the author of *The Howling Man,* and **Blooded [Anunnaki Rising]**, but she doesn't want you to confuse Blooded for just some young adult supernatural thriller with love triangles, vampires, werewolves, zombies, or dystopian societies. Blooded [Anunnaki Rising] blends the supernatural with what is perceived as mythological, historical fiction, [in which there may be more truth than fiction] while leaving readers considering the possibility that her spin on vampires might just be the real truth behind the legend.

A prolific writer of fiction, Lyn has more than a dozen books available for Kindle and book lovers, including two children's books in the "Little Book of Memories" series, which are also available in hard copy, and creative novella's that capture Lyn's diverse writing style, that include horror stories, stories filled with mystery and intrigue, ghost stories, love stories, and more.

An intuitive, hopeless romantic, Lyn loves science fiction, horror, and spirituality (but don't confuse that for being supportive of mainstream religion). Her family has a politically rich history and is tied to the American Revolution. When she's not playing World of Warcraft with her son, researching natural healing methods, or feeding the ducks in her lake, she's spinning tales of mysterious what-ifs for you.

A virtual recluse in her home, *Villa Le Paradis Sur Terre*, Lyn spends her days researching, reading, writing, and enjoying the simple things in life with her husband, such as a good cup of coffee and quiet conversation. The back of her Villa is glass from floor to ceiling and overlooks a private lake. I would say, that if ever there was truth in a statement, Lyn is living proof  that people who live in glass houses shouldn't throw stones . . . they should be writers.

You'll find Lyn Murray's Book Trailer on YouTube at the link below:

http://www.youtube.com/channel/UCxds7uuT4IMB RPLiYTNCGBQ

◇◇◇

This has been a

**Golden Panda Publishing**
Production

just GOOGLE . . . Golden Panda Publishing
. . .

https://sites.google.com/site/goldenpandapublishing/home

You'll find Lyn Murray there.

◇◇◇

Lyn's Book Trailers on YouTube –
http://www.youtube.com/channel/UCxds7uuT4IMBRPLiYTNCGBQ

## Lyn Murray's Books

Little Book of Memories, Vol. 1
Little Book of Memories, Vol. 2

One Dark Halloween Night
The Howling Man
The Tuck
Nightfall's Day
Glasses Glasses
Paula
[A Nightmare]
The 3rd Sunday of Every Month
[Mystery of White Rose Cemetery]
Who Goes There?
[The Legend of Tally Bottom Ridge]
A Case of Jitters
[Murder at Hammond Hill Rectory]
B.E.K.
[Black Eyed Kid's Phenomenon]

▼ ▼ ▼ and of course ▼ ▼ ▼

BLOODED
[Anunnaki Rising]
BLOODED – NOMADS
[Anunnaki Tribulation]
BLOODED – CINDER
[Anunnaki Armageddon]

BANE
INDIGENOUS

Weird Tales
Town at the End of Nowhere
Requiem
So . . . You Think You Know Who God Is

♦♦♦ with more on the way ♦♦♦

**The Wilde Side**
**Peter Wilde Detective**
*Coming Soon!*

You'll find Lyn's books on Amazon.com, and wherever fine books are sold.

◇◇◇

. . . Golden Panda Publishing on Google .

. .

HTTPS://SITES.GOOGLE.COM/SITE/GOLDENPAN DAPUBLISHING/HOME

YOU'LL FIND LYN MURRAY THERE.

◇◇◇

## Lyn's websites:

Just GOOGLE . . . Lyn Murray Writes
https://sites.google.com/site/lynmurraywrites/home

OR

Lyn Murray Writes 2

http://lynmurray.wix.com/lynmurray

**Our Intrepid Duo**

*(Yesterday)*

**Joe at 16**

∞

He grew up to be a Chrysler Corporation Executive,
Researcher, Artist, Author and Poet

**Lyn at 16**

∞

She grew up to be an Executive in the Film
Processing Industry, Researcher, Artist, Author,
and Poet Laureate

**The Salvation Army**

Lyn Murray's

*The Howling Man*

is brought to you

by

*Golden Panda Publishing*

**Thank You!**

I am honored that you took the time to read my book, and really hope you liked it! If you could, take a moment to let me know what you liked about it, I'd really like to know. Your feedback helps me hone my skills. I'm always looking for new ideas, and developing characters and story plots. Tell me what kind of stories you like – *I write for you!*

See ya' soon. Bye!

www.ingramcontent.com/pod-product-compliance
Lightning Source LLC
Chambersburg PA
CBHW070637290526
45790CB00001B/117